The Technique of STAINED GLASS

The Technique of
STAINED GLASS

Patrick Reyntiens

WATSON-GUPTILL PUBLICATIONS, NEW YORK

To all my friends
in Britain, Europe,
America, Africa, Asia
and Australia . . .
and to all the friends
met at Burleighfield

Copyright © 1967 and 1977 by Patrick Reyntiens
First published 1967 in Great Britain by
Batsford Books, London
Published 1967 in the United States and Canada
by Watson-Guptill Publications,
a division of Billboard Publications, Inc.,
1515 Broadway, New York, N.Y. 10036
Library of Congress Number: 67-17164
ISBN 0-8230-5525-7
First Printing, 1967
Fourth Printing, 1972
Fifth Printing, 1973
Sixth Printing, 1975
New edition, 1977

Contents

For American readers please note
the following equivalents of terms

banding = wiring
calme = came
drawing pins = thumb tacks
farriers' nails = horseshoers' nails
knapping = chipping
wide-heart = high-heart

Acknowledgment

My thanks are given to all who have helped in the preparation of this book and in particular to my colleague, Derek White for his advice, hard work and constructive criticism.

I am indebted to E. J. Nuttgens, who taught me all I know of stained glass painting techniques, and started me off on the craft with his support and encouragement. My very special thanks are due to John Piper, whose knowledge of painting, art and architecture have been an inspiration through many years of working together, and who has kindly contributed some of his photographs to this book. Thanks, too, to David Kirby, the overseer of the Liverpool Cathedral Commission.

To my friends and fellow artists in this medium who have contributed photographs and information, I am especially grateful; Ceri Richards, Brian Young, Geoffrey Clarke, Margaret Traherne, Keith New, and Tom Fairs. Also to Ann Powers, who drew all the line illustrations, the result of many hours of hard work; contributors from abroad, whose kindness enabled me to use their photographs, especially my friend Patrick Fallon, and my fellow artists Jean Barillet, Charles Marq, Paul Bony, Georg Meistermann: to these and to many others, including Laurence Madrelle, my grateful thanks. To Mrs Glass and Mrs Garland, and above all to my brother-in-law, Stephen Bally, I would like to say thanks for all the trouble and time they took over the typing.

Finally, I would thank Miss Thelma M. Nye of B. T. Batsford for her advice, patience, and sympathy in the preparation of this work, and my wife, Anne Bruce, for fifteen years of hard work, support, and encouragement since I began stained glass—years which give this book some small mandate.

P R 1967

Since this book was first published I have had more reason to thank friends from all over the world than I can remember. Most of all I would like to thank the people who bought the first edition and made the second a feasibility—and those who pointed out the mistakes, excesses and omissions.

P R 1977

Colour plates
Facing page 72 *Nuit de Noel* by Henri Matisse. Museum of Modern Art, New York, Copyright SPADEM, Paris, 1977
Facing page 96 Tribe of Joseph window, Jerusalem, by Marc Chagall. Copyright ADAGP, Paris, 1977. Photograph by Palphot Limited, Israel

Introduction

The relationship between architecture and the decorative arts is an equivocal one. Perhaps they are not at the opposite ends of the pole as they used to be, but one must admit there are very few examples of a happy relationship between the two, even in the late twentieth century, long after the 'Modern Movement' is officially dead. Stained glass, as one of the more important decorative arts, still finds itself in an alien situation, waiting to transform the interiors of buildings but only rarely being used in the right way.

Glass, being both coloured and transparent, is capable of transforming the whole of a building by a subtle unificatory process. It has the power to transmute, or to destroy, interior space. Stained glass is an environmental art, enveloping and overwhelming the spectator. It creates an atmosphere which is grasped by the eye, an envelope of experience within which the spectator moves, not a series of arresting points of contemplation.

It is in the necessary and intimate link with architecture, not in the craft, that stained glass is the direct heir of the Middle Ages. To say that stained glass as a craft is a medieval activity is to miss the point; it is the same as claiming that riding a bicycle is a twentieth-century activity or riding a horse a New Stone Age activity. Any craft, whether it is cooking or riding a bicycle, is simply the best and most economical way of doing a thing. This is why crafts are timeless and unchanging. They develop, they do not change.

The relationship of stained glass to painting and designing in general is subtle and ambiguous.

So ambiguous that there is a serious temptation for the maker of stained glass to opt out of contact with a world such as the world of painting, which is always changing and can never be pinned down to the same vocabulary of expression for more than six months at a time. Although it is stupid merely to keep up with the fashion, it is absolutely vital for the stained glass artists to have some contact with painting, because it prevents that kind of mental ossification which is the occupational hazard of the craft.

The relationship between stained glass and painting obviously varies. Broadly speaking, it is at those times when art is conceptual rather than perceptual that stained glass stands a better chance of a *rapprochement* with painting, and of deriving real benefit from such a contact. Stained glass and naturalism do not as a rule go happily together. The forms of colour and painting today, if not the language of composition, are appropriate to stained glass, and can be translated into the medium with the smallest amount of compromise, and so far from being in decline or always existing in an envelope of retrospective thinking, the art of stained glass is capable at this moment of as extended a visual exploration in its way as the art of painting. It is true that the discoveries of colour that have been made from the post-impressionists till today have not had the effect on stained glass that they have merited.

I do not deal with any history of stained glass. All the history that is important is contained in the books outlined in the bibliography. Perhaps

1 *A window by Décorchement c 1930 from the Style Déco church of Ste Odile, Paris*

it is a good thing to get acquainted with history: a sense of chronology helps a little, and therefore a brief resumé of the past sixty to seventy years may be helpful.

As regards the commissioning of windows during the last forty-five years, great opportunities have undoubtedly been lost in England, America, and France. This is largely owing to patrons and architects alike not realising that, in the succeeding phases of painting, from the post-impressionists through all the intervening movements up to the abstract expressionists, there was a real fund of talent on which they could draw and a large number of painters who would have been willing to design for stained glass had they been approached. As it is, from the whole of that period up to 1960 we have only one or two masterpieces, such as the chapel by Matisse carried out by Paul Bony (in many ways the most significant achievement of stained glass so far in the twentieth century), and the series of windows in *dalle-de-verre* to the designs of Leger, by Jean Barillet at Audincourt, and Courfaivre; then there are six windows by Rouault, also carried out by Paul Bony, and the series of executed by Paul Bony at Assy; and two churches by Georges Braque at Varangeville which only hint at the quality of the windows he might have designed: all the same, the Jesse tree window in the cliff-top church at Varangeville by Braque, where he is buried, is one of the most beautiful stained glass windows of the twentieth century. Picasso has accomplished nothing in the medium, which remains the one major means of self expression he never tried. Surveying England in the same period, the situation is even more dismal. There were practically no windows

3 *Evie Hone's east window for Eton College Chapel 1948. Almost the first instance of modern idiom of stained glass being used in England*

of interest designed by painters between the vorticist-inspired windows by Wallmark at Slough (about 1920) and the dramatic breakthrough by Evie Hone in her designs for the East Window at Eton College Chapel (1948). The Evie Hone East window at Eton, which had a late echo in the window at St Michael's Highgate also by Evie Hone, may look historic now, but when it was done it proved to be the beginning of co-operation between the eye of the painter and the eye of the artist in stained glass.

Since 1950 there have been changes in the outlook for stained glass in England. Not only have new and splendid opportunities arisen, of which Coventry and Liverpool Cathedrals are the most obvious examples, and artists of the calibre of John Piper, Ceri Richards, Geoffrey Clarke, Margaret Traherne, Brian Young designed and made windows, but there has been a spread of interest in techniques other than leaded glass; cement, concrete, polyester resin, fibreglass, and epoxy resin, have all of them produced a new range of practical possibilities and aesthetic pitfalls.

2 *A small window designed by Georges Braque (possibly the postumous rendering of a lithograph) in the Chapel of the Foundation Maeght, St Paul–de–Vence*

Since 1960 there has been a considerable amount of activity in France and Germany, as well as in England, in the commissioning of stained glass. One only has to instance the Chagall windows in Metz Cathedral; and his great series for the synagogue attached to the Hadasseh University in Jerusalem. Bissière had received commissions for Rheims and Metz Cathedras, and, in the Foundation Maeght, not far from Matisse's masterpiece at Vence, there is a window by Raoul Ubac as well as a small posthumous design by Braque rendered into glass. A large composition in *dalle-de-verre* in the Léger Museum at Biot, Var is a heavy warning against gigantism, though there are two or three further, and smaller, compositions in the Léger Museum of considerable beauty and technical originality; these are also in Dalle-de-Verre. Other artists working in the medium are Manessier, Léon Zack and Jacques Chevallier. Mention should especially be made of Paul Bony, Jean Barillet and Charles Marq who, besides being artists in their own right, are responsible for giving to the world all the work in stained glass designed by the great painters of France.

The quality of building fabrics has an appreciable effect on stained glass design. In the face of a sheer, and increasingly machine-made *matière* in building, the aesthetics of interval and division in stained glass have had to be re-thought. Until stained glass ceases to be a decorative adjunct, put into the quantity surveyor's dossier under the heading of 'supplementary art work', and is seen to be a vital constituent of some architecture, architects will not perhaps begin to consider it.

At this point I should give some word of explanation in case the impression is formed in the course of reading this book that the method of describing the various processes seems too folksy, or seems to be lifted straight out of Cobbet's *Cottage Economy*. To any criticism of this sort I would say that, in the first place, not only is the craft of stained glass, together with all the discipline of the workshop, virtually unaltered since it was invented more than a thousand years ago, but, being handmade, and having so complicated a series of contributory

factors towards its making, stained glass needs, not only a great deal of discipline and perseverance through endless trivial little details, but also incessant coaching in small economies, dodges, encouragements, and tricks of the trade that really cannot be conveyed in any other way.

The craft of any art must be taught well and become the servant of the artist in whatever he wants to say. In other words, the more disciplined the craft, the more freedom is possible for the art. The last thing I would recommend is impeccable craftsmanship for its own sake; stained glass in the recent past acquired a bad name precisely because of excessive concentration on the craft side, and as a result what was actually expressed turned out to be too boring to be considered seriously as art.

I would emphasise that there is a very real discrepancy in stained glass between the time factor of making the glass, and the time-factor or time interval of modern painting or graphic art, both of which seem to depend on the evolution of a series of images in quick succession. There is no disguising the fact that this time-lag or drag is a very real problem in all the applied arts. How can one reconcile the enormously long time it takes to make one stained glass window with the rapidity of conception and execution in painting, which is a reflection of the rapidity of movement in life today? How to reconcile these two time sequences, and keep all the vitality and immediacy in the glass during the slow process of its manufacture, depends on each individual practitioner fully realising the situation, and solving it as well as he can. One thing is certain; ignoring basic craft rules does not help in this respect.

The more efficient and, in the end, effortless the craft becomes, the more likely—given all the other factors coming into play—will stained glass be produced that has some relevance to painting and design on the one hand, and architecture on the other.

Burleighfield 1967

Preface to New Edition

It is ten years since the first edition of this work was published, and much has happened within the world of stained glass during that time.

Nowadays, how-to-do-it books abound—do-it-yourself books too—and stained glass is no exception; there are some hundreds of stained glass do-it-yourself books. If this is the case, why, I ask myself, should I try to reissue *The Technique of Stained Glass*, especially since readers of the previous edition will scarcely fail to notice that the sections on epoxy resins, *dalle-de-verre,* and resin-bonded glass without lead, have been removed altogether. Yet I think the reissue of the book is necessary because I have learnt a great deal in the past ten years that I think is of importance to everyone—not only to myself.

Firstly I have come to a most definite conclusion that lead-bonded glass is the only medium that is of interest to me. Not only is this medium the most flexible and viable but it is the *only* medium of stained glass that does not run the risk of being encapsulated in technique and technical problems. In a predominantly technological age, a new technical solution, such as a new machine, is taken to be the saving of the situation. I want to avoid giving the impression that I am *against* new techniques, but at the same time I wish to emphasise that *vision,* the end in sight, is of inestimably more value than techniques, the means, and that, paradoxically, if I did not believe this very strongly, I should not have attempted a reissue of this technical book. The object is to release the reader from technical complications so that vision, or the realisation of vision, through simple means, is possible. This alone counts.

Secondly the world has changed much in the last ten years. In 1967 there were enormous projects either being completed or about to be completed (I instance Coventry, Liverpool, and San Francisco cathedrals) which by stealing the attention of the public, built up an expectation of an 'era of stained glass' which nowhere appeared except in great glory in Federal Germany.

The idea that many individuals could make modestly sized panels for homes and domestic situations seemed malapropos and quaint at the time. The great commodity-job seemed the ideal—hundreds of cathedrals. Yet if stained glass is going to attain a status of more than a minor decorative art perhaps the best road to this is not of *few* people doing physically colossal work, both mopping the market and the attention of the public, but of *many* people producing personal statements in glass: statements depending on a changing vision—a vision in a constant state of *re*vision in fact. This will alone produce the matrix out of which a new style may crystallise if it only persists for a few years.

It is to these individuals that I dedicate this book; and I am aware through my travels and contacts that they reside mostly in America, Canada and Australia.

I mentioned earlier the German achievement. This is the greatest of the twentieth century's achievements in the medium of leaded glass.

The political, economic, and spiritual reasons for this truly staggering oeuvre are so obvious as to be not worth explaining. I would like to point out, however, *one* discrepancy which I think has not been taken into account. Germany always has displayed a supreme genius for art 'on a public scale', i.e. as a generally accepted art-form for the public. We can see this looking back into history through the rococo and then the baroque, through high gothic to the romanesque. It is on *that* tradition of public acceptance that Germany's achievement in the twentieth century is founded, art being an expression of social cohesion. However, contrasted to the German situation, which has grave limitations in one direction, is the situation in the countries I mention above, where the art of stained glass is undergoing a birth rather than a rebirth. There the emphasis is almost entirely on the small scale personal effort, producing a myriad of achievements, each of unique style (or lack of it) owing to the psychological assumptions governing the nature and use of art. The possibility of small-scale private achievement is to all intents and purposes impossible in Germany, whereas it is the norm in America. Therefore Americans should be very careful not to support in America the outer mannerisms of the German achievement and hope to build a personal style on them. It won't work. I put this warning in because some of you may think that having seemed to weigh heavily against the German achievement in the Preface, it is perverse of me to illustrate this book so fully with German photographs. I think not, having in mind Gerard Manly Hopkins' dictum 'admire and do otherwise'. If it works for poets it should work for stained glass artists. Everyone must be themselves, although we can all learn from one another.

I should like to end on a personal note. When I wrote this book in 1967 the Educational Institute which I and my wife founded and which later became world famous as *Burleighfield*, had only just begun; it was an empirical thing with no theory behind it—only practice. Now that *Burleighfield*, as hundreds knew it, is destroyed, and the furniture and library dispersed, the vision of the place still persists. A new international school of stained glass is in the course of construction at Beaconsfield, not far away, and soon we hope to receive people there who would, in happier times, have come to see us and learn in *Burleighfield*.

I should so much like to thank Brian Clark for his generosity in making the photographs of German glass available to me. I confess I have never been to Germany except on one-day flights to Düsseldorf to buy glass from Herr Becker (whom God preserve) since the late fifties. I look forward to going there when the labour of revising this book is over.

Again I must thank Thelma M. Nye for her unfailing patience in putting up with an author caught recently in what seemed like the hazards of war, and of being a refugee.

I dedicate this second edition of my book to Robert, Ed, Peter, Stewart, Yosh, Doreen, Cedar, Big Daddy, Ludibaby, Freddie, Greg, Jessica, and *all* who have visited Burleighfield and may have made, incidentally, the planning of a second edition a *sine qua non*.

PR 1977

The Studio

Stained glass is apt to make more chaos and mess than any other art. Moreover, like that of sculpture, it is one of the dustiest occupations, having kiln dust, glass dust, cement dust, black lead, and vegetable black dust, to say nothing of powdered resin, powder paint, and dust from heaters. So it is essential to keep things in order, and of course the smaller the studio area within which to manœuvre, the more important it is to keep it tidy, and to keep everything clean. It is therefore helpful to set aside a certain time each day to do the routine jobs.

There is a right and natural relationship between work and comfort. An atmosphere of being ill at ease, of battling against circumstances and odds, is only a romantic and rather unprofessional reflection of the state of uncertainty that is sometimes inside the person. So many people purposely make themselves uncomfortable and seem to get into uncomfortable positions and attitudes, and tolerate the most absurd impediments. The *glass* is the important image you are creating in the studio, not the projected image of your being busy at work.

You cannot create in discomfort. Discomfort is inefficient and a waste of labour and time and, in the end, of money.

Make certain that the benches are at a convenient height, that things are easily get-at-able, and that there is a logical sequence to the layout of the studio. The chairs which are there to rest in and sit down on should be comfortable, the heating adequate, and the tea- or coffee-making

equipment clean and efficient. I cannot overstress the real contributory nature of being comfortable. Comfort, not ease, is an essential condition for creation in stained glass.

Personal side
The previous remarks are applicable to craftsmen either in partnership or alone, but if the student takes up stained glass as a career, he will have to go into a large studio and learn to co-operate. If he is untidy and undisciplined, he is a menace to everyone else. The atmosphere of a studio where more than one person is working should be no different in seriousness of intent from, say, a highly organised chemistry laboratory.

It is essential to have sharp tools and the right tools ready to hand, the right raw materials, and work benches, made to a convenient height, which are stable and firm, and do not tip up.

All benches and tables should be essentially moveable in the central area of the studio.

Decide whether or not such equipment as tables and waste-bins are more easily managed on castors. I have made a rule based on the observation that anything that needs two people to lift and carry, if on wheels, only needs one person.

Decide on the disposition of light. Contrary to what might be supposed, there is no need for a great deal of electric light in the studio. By correctly placing the main lights and by making use of extendable or flexible lamp standards, electricity bills can be cut by a quarter.

4 *Showing set-up for stained glass with mullions spaced and wooden battens in place in the brackets. Note lighting*

5 *Lead-lined plate glass set up on mullions forming total composition wall at end of studio, prior to putting on stained glass*

Decide on the main rabbit-runs of the studio, and have a proper sequence of work from the cartooning, to the cutting, to the leading and cementing, so that the same path is not crossed too many times.

All these decisions, together with the neatness of the glass and the lead racks, have a real bearing on the quality of a window, because, when a *commission* has to be carried out, as opposed to an art school exercise, time, an important economic factor, is involved.

Setting up the studio

In no other art or craft is the shape, size, and disposition of the studio so important as in stained glass. As well as being a place to work in, the stained glass studio has to be constructed rather like the box of a box camera. That is, it has to have only one source of light to work by.

I am aware that when you first set up a studio, there is always the dream of an ideal, but generally one has to make do with what is available. However, stables, garages, flats, outhouses of any sort, can make adequate accommodation.

If you are lucky enough to have a studio built to your own specification, or have a very large building to use as a studio, the following plan would be well worth considering.

Main studio

The main part of the studio should be as large as possible. It should be deep, with no windows on either side, but a large window taking up the full height and breadth of the end wall; this window should, ideally, be large enough to take the most ambitious window you are ever likely to make. As few stained glass windows are made and fixed in such a position that you have to appreciate them with your nose to the glass, it is essential to be able to climb down from your ladder or scaffold from time to time to view the work from a distance.

It is most important to have good ventilation in this large window, as all the heat of the studio travels to the roof, and if it cannot escape it collects and melts the wax or plasticine holding the glass whilst it is being painted. The ventilation should be controllable, because in winter precisely the opposite may happen, especially if the work is left over-night: the cold makes the wax or plasticine so brittle that the glass is apt to lose adhesion and fall down.

The whole of the wall to the left or right of the studio window (at right angles to it) is best lined with strawboard, so that sketches and cartoons can quickly be pinned on to it for reference. If you are doing a series of windows it is quite a good idea to put the cartoons of the previous window and the one to follow, either side of the window you are working on, to see how they harmonise together. Usually only one wall can be utilised for cartoons, because the other is taken up with the racks for antique glass. The placing of these racks here is important, as it enables the selection of glass to be made with the stained glass you are working on up against the light. An instant comparison between the colour in the window and the colour that is selected is thus possible. Having selected the glass in this way each sheet can be returned to its home rack, keeping the studio tidy and free from odd bits of glass and sheets of glass.

A wash-basin and a supply of running water in the studio are absolutely essential.

Kiln room

It is most important to have the kiln in a separate room because the mess and heat and general discomfort are too much to have in the same place as the stained glass window. Firing is, on the whole, tricky work, and the time sequences are very short (ten minutes or under; sometimes as little as half a minute), and whoever is doing the firing should not be distracted from paying attention to the timing. The kiln room should be reasonably insulated and free from draughts, as these upset the working of the kiln. It should be wide and large enough to give adequate room to work the kiln with the long two-handed key or tool that is used to withdraw the trays of glass. It should also be big enough to contain two benches of good size, so that the kiln trays may be laid out with glass and not get muddled up with one another.

Make sure the doorway to the kiln room is of sufficient width; many trays have come to grief through being knocked up against a doorpost.

Glazing room

A separate room for glazing is advisable, but is by no means essential. It should be large enough to have either one very big bench in the centre, or two or three benches fixed to the wall. A central bench is preferable because if there is an extra large panel, or extra wide window, the far side can be reached without undue physical effort and stretching. A good proportion of bench is 4·5 m long × 2·5–3 m wide (15 ft long × 9–10 ft wide). If there is only room for a glazing bench in the studio proper I advise it to be in the form of a simple heavy table top on trestles. This can then be taken down and stacked when not in use. There are other advantages of a removable, or movable, glazing bench which will appear in due course in this book.

Cementing room

Adjoining the glazing room, and yet farther away from the studio, should be a small room set aside for cementing. This can be an outhouse made of wood. The act of cementing keeps the cementer warm enough in winter without heating. This small room or shed should be kept locked, as some of the ingredients in stained glass cement are dangerously poisonous. There should also be a good stout bench, and places to store such things as boiled oil and whitening, and to keep out of harm's way red lead. (The use of red lead is illegal in the USA.) This room could conceivably also be used for storing in a safe place other dangerous or toxic substances used occasionally in stained glass, such as hydrofluoric acid, acetic acid, acetone, wood alcohol, and white acid. In the same room there should also be either a rack or an inclined wooden board on which to leave the panels of stained glass during the process of cementing. This room may be used for any other unusually messy jobs that have to be done from time to time.

Aciding compound

Away from the studio, and away from general

contact with people or animals, should be built an aciding compound, perhaps 2·5 m × 2·5 m (8 ft × 8 ft), with a concrete washable floor, a large polythene tub, and a bench on which can be put one or more plastic developing trays. The compound should be open to the weather, so that the fumes of the hydrofluoric acid that is used to etch the glass can escape straight away. Fumes of hydrofluoric acid are stronger than those of most acids, and are extremely dangerous. The compound can be roofed against the weather, either with wood or corrugated polythene. Metal is not quite so good.

Packing shed
A separate shed for packing and unpacking is very useful, as the last place one wants to do this is in the actual working area. It is inconceivable, to anyone who has not had a studio of his own, how much packing material accumulates in a very short time. Usually at least half is thrown away but boxes, crates, wood-wool, straw, corrugated cardboard, and paper are all useful and can be stored. It is as well to have this shed some little way away from the studio, as the risk of fire is high and a cigarette smoked carelessly whilst packing can destroy one's life's work.

The roof over the main studio, or the lean-to roofs of the subsidiary rooms, are extremely useful for storing all the cutlines, plans, cartoons, working drawings and cardboard cylinders that accumulate in the studio in no time at all.

Drawing room
If possible, it is ideal to have a good room for setting out cutlines, and for drawing cartoons and preparing sketches. This can be fitted in at the end of the studio above the entrance, as a kind of gallery, so as not to impede the view of any window which is being worked on. I realise most people do not have studios large enough to accommodate a special cartooning area so this has to be done in the main space. However, remember that Magritte did all his painting in the kitchen whilst his wife was cooking.

Business room
Finally, a word of advice on paper work. A room

is needed for this. A room where all the correspondence can be attended to, and the files kept. Remember that owing to the complexity of the set-up of stained glass, there is far more paper work attached to it, and in many more different directions, than in any other art or craft. The fatal thing is to get the paper work muddled up with the artistic work. The two must be kept apart, and time must be set aside for answering letters, preparing estimates and paying bills. If this is not kept to a strict routine, the resulting chaos and anxiety will have a disastrous effect on the quality of the work in hand. All that is needed in this room is a chair and a table, and a bookshelf on which to put the filing boxes.

5(a) *A panel designed by Ludwig Schaffrath photographed in the studio of Dr Oidtmann*

18

Telephone

The telephone unfortunately has to be in the studio as well as in the office.

Studio furniture

The main item of studio furniture is the easel, or device for holding glass.

The easel

Against the large window I have installed a pair of industrial rails, the whole width of the window and about 45 cm (18 in.) inside; the mullions are suspended from these rails individually on bogies, rather like a sliding door, and are sectioned as shown in the diagram. They stretch the whole height of the studio and are fixed by means of grub-screw seatings to rails at floor level. At the top, on one end, there is a section of the industrial rail that removes so that the bogies holding the mullions can be taken out and repaired when necessary. There is enough tolerance in the length of the mullions to be able to swing them sideways off their seating to take them out of the industrial rails altogether. Unless locked by the grub-screws at the bottom, they are free to travel laterally, into any required position. Mullions can quickly and easily be transferred to the front or the back rail if more are needed, or all mullions to one rail or the other. Conversely, if the whole width of the studio is needed the mullions not needed can either be taken away and stored, or stacked well back on both sides of the large window, but remember that mullions, when stacked together, are apt to take up a considerable amount of space and reduce the working area of light.

Mullions

Each mullion is equipped with facilities to take three methods of setting up the glass. Usually one method is enough; but owing to various improvements over the years, the mullions that are illustrated can now cope with:

1 large easels of wood enclosing plate glass and counter-weighted over sprockets or pulleys;
2 individual pieces of plate glass corresponding to the sizes of the panels being worked on;

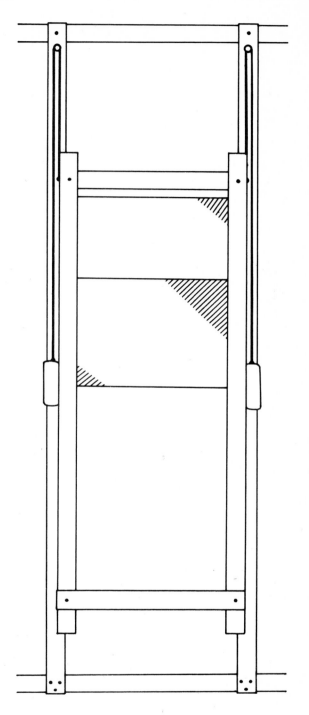

6 *The easel with counter-weights*

3 individual pieces of plate glass organized together into a system.

These methods are discussed more fully on pages 39–45.

If any, or all, of these methods are adopted, it is important to have the mullions leaning outwards at an angle of 85° or so, and the rails top and bottom sited accordingly. In this way any glass on the easel will not tend to be loosened and dragged off by gravity.

For the last method, which I have adopted after years of experiment, I have invented a system that meets all these requirements.

On the face of the mullions, long iron tubes of 25 mm (1 in.) diameter are fixed on mounts (see diagram). They stop short of the bottom of the mullions by 152 mm (6 in.) so that the shoe-bracket can be slipped on from underneath. The brackets consist of two parts: (1) a ring which fits over the iron tube and is held in place by a grub-screw (the ring is split at the back to allow it to travel up the tube without fouling the mounts); and (2) a bracket made of hollow 25 mm × 25 mm (1 in. × 1 in.) iron with a couple of grub-screws at either end in seatings on the top side. This bracket is welded on to the previous unit so that their axes are at right angles, and the weld is made firmer by the braces of metal. The hollow side of the second unit faces in towards the studio, and the whole unit is free to slide the length of the mullion, which in its turn is free to slide from side to side on the industrial rails.

Unplaned wooden battens are inserted in the metal holdings, aligned up, with 6 mm to 3 mm ($\frac{1}{4}$ in. to $\frac{1}{8}$ in.) of wood standing proud. The face of the wood is then finished with 38 mm ($1\frac{1}{2}$ in.) dome-headed screws, each of which, round its shaft, has a rubber collar or washer, made of cut-up high-pressure gas tubing perhaps, about 6 mm ($\frac{1}{4}$ in.) long. These washered screws are placed to bear the weight of a panel of plate glass.

If the battens of wood are placed accurately in the brackets, and the whole apparatus is carefully aligned so that when the interval between the battens is equal to the interval of individual pieces

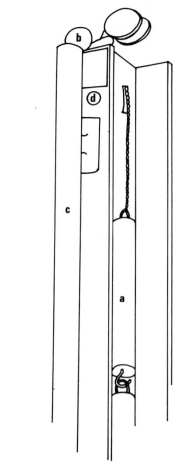

7 *Mullion showing*
   a *counter-weight on chains over sprocket* (d)
   b *overhead industrial bogies*
   c *vertical fitment for taking brackets holding horizontal battens*

of plate glass, and the bracket grub-screws are locked into position, there is a complete system which looks rather like a climbing grid in a gymnasium. It will enable the glass panels to be taken out and put back, but kept in their position in the window, on the wooden battens, by the pressure of the rubber tubing on the screws top and bottom. As an additional safety precaution, brass cuphooks, L-shaped, 15 mm ($\frac{1}{2}$ in.), can be screwed in and turned over the edge of the glass at the top of each panel. It is best to set up this easel system with the series of panes of plate glass which you are actually going to use, as the slightest variation in size can tend to stiffness of extraction. A correctly sized pane of glass as a gauge is quite essential.

Setting up an entire window in this way will take perhaps a morning or even a whole day—but for a large job that is going to be worked on for many weeks, it is time well spent.

Tracery technique

Using the above method of setting up glass, it is quite easy to set up tracery in the same way. Make a wall of plate glass and hang in front of it a previously cut out full-sized black paper mask of the whole tracery. Adhesive tape will keep it in position on the glass. With a chinagraph pencil trace inside the mask holes, on to the plate glass, the outlines of the tracery and their relationships to one another. Number these. Remove the mask and the glass. Lead-line the glass from the appropriate tracery outline and then, hanging the mask against the mullion, *first* this time, in the exact position that it was during the marking, reimpose the glass wall, lead-lined, on the mask carefully piercing the black paper with a cross-cut with a sharp knife where the washered screws or cuphooks occur. Plasticine the intersections of the lead-lines and stick on to the plastircine the cut antique glass.

Storage of glass panels

Against the studio wall covered with strawboard, it is as well to have a storage unit made for the individual panels of glass when they are not being worked on. This storage unit can be used as a low bench for setting out on, for sitting on, and for an extra height to stand on whilst cartooning. As shown in the diagram it is a primitive creation, capable of improvement. The main fault is that the lead-lines on the back of the glass are apt to be scraped off by the wooden battens supporting the glass. The glass, unless guided tends to go in slightly sideways and usually gets stuck, and if the racks are not sufficiently high, i.e. have at least an inch of space in which to manœuvre, the plating that may be on top of the antique glass can be pushed off and smashed in the process of

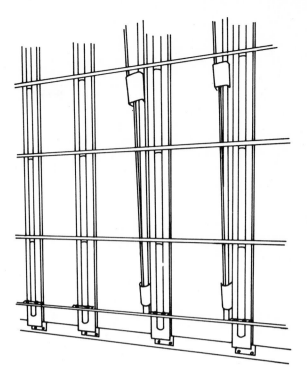

8 *Mullions set up ready for work*

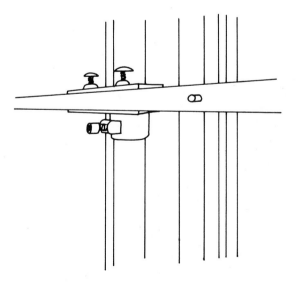

9 *Sliding bracket holding horizontal battens*

21

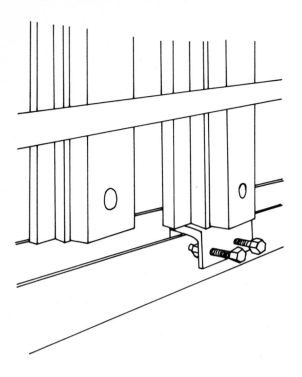

10 *Detail of grub-screw anchor fixing to floor rail*

sliding the panels into the rack. Therefore have have plenty of space for the panel of glass to move in.

The cartoon wall

If the studio is 4·8 m (16 ft) high or more, which it ought to be, there is quite a problem in getting to the top of the walls and window to work on the cartoon and on the glass. Along the cartoon wall I had a catwalk made, which was suspended from the roof and supported on two brackets, well wide of the cartoon wall. This meant that there was ample room to thread the cartoons up under the catwalk between the iron of the catwalk and the cartoon wall.

The catwalk is placed so that there is room to stretch one's arms above one's head a little. At the same time, it is not just so low as to become an impediment to anyone wishing to work below. Removable duckboards are placed in the gangplank space; these can be removed when you wish to look at a whole cartoon or cutline.

A simpler, but far less accurate way of hoisting cartoons to ceiling height is to have a series of free-moving battens which are suspended on string threaded through pulleys at the top of the wall. The cartoons are then drawing-pinned to the battens along the top, and the batten is taken up to the height of the wall by pulling the string. If there is more than one batten the cartoons are then aligned and set out ready for working on or for cut-lining off. The disadvantages of this system are that:

1 On the whole it is inaccurate, because it is difficult to align them and set them square. (This may not be too much of a worry if the window is to be placed in old stonework, which can stand a little inaccuracy but work done in modern metal and concrete settings has to be very accurately set up.)
2 The pulleys go wrong, the string gets caught up in them, and the cartoon gets stuck. Sometimes, owing to rough usage and the string getting frayed, the whole batten and cartoon comes down on one's head in the process of working.
3 Limitations of width. These battens are only effective with a series of upright single lights of a maximum width of 0·9 m (3 ft) unattached to one another. Large cartoons, perhaps up to 4·5 m (15 ft) wide, are practically impossible to handle on a series of independent battens.

In addition to a catwalk against the cartooning wall, some system of constructing a temporary working area across the window space so as to work on the glass would be of advantage. I have used carpenter's or builders' trestles with boards across them, and would recommend some kind of platform. The alternative is to use a step-ladder or a ladder leaning on a rail inserted in the *studio* side of the industrial rails holding the mullions at the top. Either using a ladder or a step-ladder the work is precarious and risky, and there is no place to put pallette or brushes, thereby forcing the painter to come down the ladder to ground level, up again to paint—a tedious process, and tiring on the legs after a couple of days.

Table

A general-purpose table in the middle of the studio is a good idea. This can have drawers in it for tools at one end, and brushes at the other. If more table space is needed, there can be two tables, each perhaps as big as an old-fashioned kitchen table, and both on castors. The lower one can slide under the higher one when not in use. A set of chocks to bring the lower table up to the height of the taller one is useful. Two or three waste bins on wheels are essential.

Other equipment

A small bookshelf in the studio is useful for books of reference, and another for paints, glue and so on.

A small nest of drawers is recommended. Industrial metal drawer units are best: there are so many small items such as screws, nails, electrical fittings, plasticine, beeswax, locks and bolts, to keep tidy and close at hand, that this nest of drawers is almost the most essential thing in the studio after the easel system.

Two or three duckboards, to stand on when cutting and glazing, are very useful; not only do they prevent the glass chips from being crunched underfoot, but they also prevent your feet getting cold and since almost all the work that is done in the studio is done standing, this is an important factor to consider.

Glass racks

On the opposite wall of the studio to the cartoon wall is the glass rack for antique glass. This should be very soundly constructed out of wood, firmly secured to a wall or the floor, and the correct size. French and German glass is approximately 86 cm × 91 cm (34 in. × 36 in.) and English is 61 cm × 45 cm (24 in. × 18 in. American glass is approximately the same. There must of course be a certain amount of leeway in the height and depth of the racks. Although the glass should sit well back into the rack, so that there are no edges sticking out on which to catch the face or the back of the hand, try to avoid having too deep a rack, because if, after a while, the glass breaks in the rack and little pieces of glass come

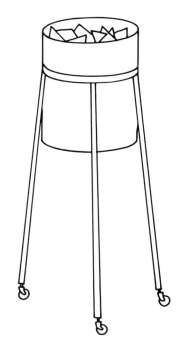

11 *Waste bin on wheels*

off, they will all tend to be pushed to the rear of the rack. When this happens it is best to remember that unless these pieces are removed straight away, they will prevent fresh glass being pushed right home, and they may well start fractures in the fresh glass, and cause additional breakages.

The width of each rack individually should never be more than 152 mm (6 in.). If it is more, the tendency will be to push too much glass into the compartment, at the risk of cracking and breakages.

When building a glass rack, make certain that if the floor is boarded the grain runs from front to rear of the rack, NOT ACROSS. Glass is easier to slide in and out when it runs with the grain than when it runs across it.

It is essential to have the divisions between each compartment of the glass rack constructed of slats 38 mm × 38 mm (1½ in. × 1½ in.) running from front to back, i.e. 38 mm (1½ in.) in depth— 15 mm (½ in.) with flat face to you. These slats should be placed at intervals of 88 mm (3½ in.)

23

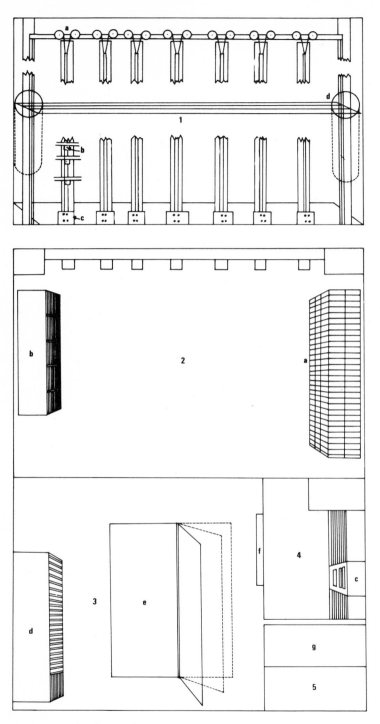

1 *elevation of mullions*
2 *main studio area*
3 *glazing room*
4 *firing room*
5 *cementing room*

a *glass rack*
b *storage rack for plate glass*
c *kiln*
d *side glazing bench*
e *main glazing bench*
f *lead racks*
g *cementing table*

12 *Plan of the ideal studio*

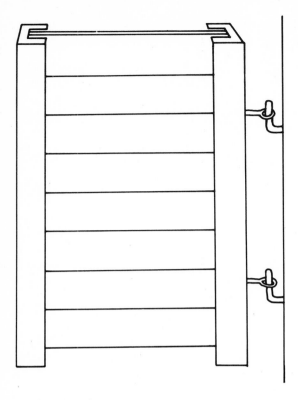

13 Sample rack

in order to be able to reach through from one compartment to the other to release the glass when it gets jammed together, or bits get broken off that have to be extracted from the back.

The glass storage racks should never be placed above head height in the ordinary studio, as it is impossible to see what one is doing, and there is a grave risk of pieces of glass flying out and causing serious injury.

Additional racks
In addition to the large racks, it is essential to have smaller racks, so as to keep the half-sheets and smaller pieces of glass separately.

These are sometimes placed on top of the large racks, but this is too high; such racks are better on their own, at floor level, because of the danger of falling pieces when selecting glass. If a rack is at floor level, there is enough space on top of it to place boxes in which the smallest pieces of

glass, left over from past work, can be stored; one box to each colour.

At the window end of the stained glass racks, there should be a colour chart of small samples of glass, which correspond in position with the glass in the racks. The glass racks should be numbered, and the appropriate numbers written against the sample, together with the amount of sheets in the rack. A complete visual inventory of the glass racks is then conveniently to hand.

If you are teaching any number of students and even if you have assistants who are uneconomical in their use of glass it is best to mark on a small sticker the retail price of any particular piece of glass (perhaps with its re-ordering number as well) so that people realise the real worth of what they are handling.

The equipment and organisation of the individual auxiliary rooms round the main studio is dealt with under the appropriate chapters.

Lighting
Lighting in general can be kept to a minimum. My studio is fitted with artificial light in the window space. Not only is it easy to work at night on the first phase of the glass painting, but it is essential to have artificial light for the execution of artificially lit stained glass murals. In England cold cathode tubing, colour matching or white, is the best kind to use. The cold cathode tubes are 2·5 m (7 ft 6 in.) long and extremely thin, and two of them vertically end to end placed on the inside face of each mullion of the outer window will illuminate the whole height of the studio. It is comparatively easy to fit cold cathode tubes to the mullions of the outer studio windows, though they may have to be protected from human contact more than other electrical apparatus, the electrical pressure needed to work them being 3000 volts.

If you are working on a mural, it is essential to have strawboard panels, painted white on the inside, which can simply be placed in the window areas, thus blocking out all natural light, and enabling you to work with the closest possible facsimile of the conditions under which the mural will be seen. It is essential when carrying out an artificially-lit stained glass mural to get the exact type of fluorescent glass tube that is going to be used *in situ*. Otherwise you will get a nasty shock when you see the final results. Fluorescent light has a general habit of blanching out colours. Colours that have looked rich and harmonious in the studio, look bleached and meagre under fluorescent light. This particularly applies to neutral colours.

A series of local lights is all that is needed for the rest of the studio and the glazing and cementing sheds. All the work that can be done in the studio in the evening is of a small local nature, i.e. cutting, cutlining and sticking glass on to plate glass. Four power points in the studio, and one two-way adaptor to each power point are all that is needed. All lights should be flexible, portable, and adaptable. Anglepoise lamps or wall-bracket angle lamps are admirable.

If possible, the floor of the studio should be made of wood, uncovered. Linoleum is a luxury which quickly becomes spoilt. Vinyl plastic flooring is satisfactory. Concrete should be covered with boards or plastic—or a compound magnesite covering. Unsurfaced concrete, as well as being cold in winter and hard on the feet, is dangerous should a piece of glass be dropped on it; the glass shatters in all directions.

Office discipline

One word about office discipline. More businesses go wrong through slack office discipline than any other cause. If you are not by nature disciplined in the office, and many craftsmen are not, using up all their organising energy in their craft, enlist the help of someone who is. Stained glass before very long becomes a business, not in the sense that it is done solely to make money, but that the administration becomes extremely complex if any large commissions are carried out. Keep files tidy and in order, with a file for each job.

Set aside time for writing letters, and try to pay your bills promptly. An accountant is a great help in this.

Insurance

A word of advice:

1 Always work through a broker, he will set you the lowest terms.
2 Terms will be reduced as time goes on, by the insurance firm's increasing confidence in your ability not to smash glass.
3 If ALL the insurance is handled by one firm then the transportation insurance may be set off against the total insurance premiums.
4 Insure against the possible things: Comprehensive to studio (i.e. fire, theft, loss, breakage). Accidents to self and employees. Compensation against loss of earnings in case of fire, illness, etc.
5 The crucial point of handing over insurance is a most important consideration. I always prefer to hand over just outside the studio, charging the price of glass *ex-works* (without including fixing, insurance and transport). But this point of transfer or exchange must be detailed with extreme precision otherwise claims will not be entertained. It is bad policy to extend one's insurance to any period *longer* than delivery to site. On site anything may happen, and it is up to the builder or fixer to be responsible for what goes on. If he is insuring he *will* be responsible and what is more to the point is that you will not be asked to re-create, artistically, a composition that you have already completed. There is no greater mental fatigue than to be asked to do this.

It is a melancholy fate that awaits the stained the glass designer and maker, who seems to devote the first half of his life to making original windows, only to have the second half interspersed with urgently required repairs to his own work of decades ago. I certainly seem to have arrived at this stage of my life.

Choice and Storage of Glass

Any kind of flat glass, provided it is not too thick and therefore too heavy, can be used in stained glass. It entirely depends on what the artist wants to say in the final window. Certainly it would be most unwise not to investigate every possibility of commercial glass, and a visit to a large glass wholesaler's warehouse is essential to the completion of a stained glass training. Any plate glass, frosted glass, called in the trade 'obscured glass', black or white glass, ribbed, embossed, decorated sheet, and commercial coloured glass can be used.

Though there is no reason for not using commercial glass if you want to, the glass which, from the mid-nineteenth century, has been especially made for the use of stained glass artists is the main raw material of your art.

It can be divided into the following categories:

1 *Crown glass* This consists of a small blob of glass that has been collected on the end of the glass-blower's pipe. Instead of being blown into a bubble, it is spun round on its own axis, centrifugal force pulling out the blob till it is a spinning disc, any size in diameter up to 1·5 m (5 ft) depending on the amount of glass originally in the blob. It is thought that ancient glass may have been made in this way. Certainly the examination of pieces of thirteenth-century glass in France leads to this conclusion.

The disc is broken off the glass-maker's rod, and becomes a thin disc with a thick knotted knob in the middle. The thin glass was much used in

14 *Blowing glass in the twelfth century. Rabanus Maurus* AD *1023 Monte Cassino Library*

the seventeenth and eighteenth centuries for window-panes; and the knobby irregular part in the middle was sold off cheaply and used in the poorer houses, public houses, and farm buildings; this part of the crown was known as bullion. Crown glass is sometimes used in stained glass today, but usually it is artistically indigestible, because of its arty-crafty overtones.

To break into a crown, and use pieces of it, unless there is a definite end in mind, is wasteful.

15 Blowing glass in the early fifteenth century. 'De Universo' AD 1425 Vatican Library

2 *Norman slab* Both the name and the method of producing this glass is a product of the nineteenth century romantic imagination. When the technique of hand glass-blowing was revived in the nineteenth century, specially for the purposes of stained glass, there was a demand for rough, irregular, and glinting pieces of glass to be put into lead. Norman slab met this need. It is made by blowing a bubble of glass into a four-sided rectangular bottle. After the bulb of excess glass has been cut off from the top, the bottle is removed from the mould, smartly tapped at the corners, and falls apart into four sides, each about 175 mm × 125 mm (7 in. × 5 in.), and a bottom 125 mm × 125 mm (5 in. × 5 in.).

Norman slabs are very difficult to handle in stained glass, because of the extreme irregularity of their thickness. The edges of the slabs are very thin, yet the middle of the slabs can be up to 15 mm ($\frac{1}{2}$ in.) thick. If you wish to cut a Norman slab down the middle, it is impossible to do so cleanly without giving the slab a tap so smart that it usually shatters. It is almost impossible to lead up even if it does survive the kiln. It is practically impossible to obtain slab glass any more. Occasion-ally some comes on the market when an elderly stained-glass artist dies in England. Hartley-Wood of Sunderland have abandoned making slab except to special order. They retain the means to make it but owing to minimal demand they do not market it commercially.

3 *Crossed slab*, or *pressed slab*, is very similar to Norman slab, but is made on a different principle. The molten glass is rolled out on an iron table by means of an iron rolling-pin. Both the table and the pin are indented in various ways, which marks the slab and presses it into an irregular-surfaced piece of glass. This glass is practically unobtainable, and was never sufficiently stable to be fired.

4 *Pâte de verre*: a variant of pressed slab, which was brought to an expensive and unbelievable degree of finesse by the French Art Déco artist Décorchement is to be seen in the church of St Odile, Porte de Champeret, Paris. Pâte de verre consists of designs being made by means of heating and pressing together thousands of small pieces and scintillae of different coloured glasses—the resultant multi-coloured fusing together is almost transparent painting. The examples, huge in extent, in St Odile, are stupifying.

5 *Antique glass* is the normal staple glass used in all stained glass work. Both the name and the method of making the glass are a nineteenth-century invention, based on the idea that this method was supposed to have been used in the past to make stained glass, hence the name 'antique'.

Antique glass is made by blowing a large-sized bubble of glass, which is then pierced at the end, and at the same time gently swung from side to side, or spun, to prevent the hollow cylinder (as the glass has become) from falling in and collapsing on itself. When the cylinder is sufficiently firm to stand upright by itself, the top is broken off by means of a filament of molten glass being wrapped round the position where the crack is needed. The cylinders, or muffs, are then split down the side by a single straight-line diamond-cut, and are turned over on their sides, afterwards going through a long annealing process on a conveyor belt. At the end of half a day of gentle heat they lie down flat and lose their high degree of temper sufficiently to be used with safety in the stained glass studio.

Antique glass is coloured by means of metal oxides; the exact amount and proportion remain the secret of the chemist. It depends on the degree of sensitivity and intuition of the chemist in the factory as to whether good colours are produced or crude and obvious ones.

The following colours are obtained by the metallic oxides indicated:

Blue	cobalt oxide, and combinations of cobalt and chromium
Red	selenium in combination with *cadmium* and copper salts
Red-pink (*Gold-pink*)	manganese oxide, gold oxide; this can vary between deep cherry red and light camellia pink; extremely expensive.
Purple	manganese in conjunction with cobalt blue
Yellow	selenium and chromium in conjunction with cadmium salts
Sulphur yellow	sodium
Black	concentrated copper salts
Green	copper and chromium salts

Simple single colours, with the colour spread throughout the substance of the glass, are known as 'pot' glass (the 'pot' being the steel-lined vat where the molten glass is kept in flux during the blowing of the antique) because it only needs to be made from one pot of one colour.

There is another variant on antique known as 'flash' glass (French = *plaquée*; German = *Überfang*) which is made of a large amount of base colour, generally very lightly coloured, fused onto a thin film of stronger colour, usually red, blue or green; the two layers of glass are blown out together, by the blower first collecting a very small amount of deep colour on his blow-pipe and then progressively building up a thick layer base (weak-toned) colour or white. Usually he

has to dip his blow-pipe in two or three successive times. The antique taken from this bubble has a layer of strong colour on top of a thicker layer of weak colour.

Certain colours are essentially flashed glass. Red is nearly always flashed when it is not coloured with selenium. Greens are frequently flashed. Blues may or may not be.

The French, as a rule, are far more adventurous in producing flashed glass, having besides red-on-white, red-on-blue, red-on-yellow (all of which are made well in England, too), red-on-rose-pink, and red-on-light-green, red-on-deep-blue, and red on violet.

When the flashed glass is cooled and the sheet is held up, it can be seen that the colour changes from the base colour to the flash colour quite considerably. One way in which you can always tell whether glass has a flash on it or not, is to chip one edge of the glass; or else cut a small piece off the sheet and have a look through it on edge against the light; and there you may see if it is a white glass with a ruby or blue flash, or whatever flash colour has been used. On a white glass you can see just the white glass with a thin edge, the thickness of the flash. Similarly if you have a blue pot glass, with a ruby flash on it, it is easier to see the blue base sideways, though the glass will appear red when you look view-ways through it.

On the whole, the English are best at greens and reds; the French on all blues, browns, and yellowish greens; the Germans on ochre, grey, white, dull bottle greens, green-blues, deep blues and deep reds, and, above all, the marvellous series of opaque and opalescent colours which they have themselves invented.

It is not at all a bad thing, when ordering glass, to ask for a job-lot of any particular colour you are interested in. Job-lots cost about one-third the amount of ordinary antique, and contain a large number of variants on greys or greens or blues, and can be a very valuable way of stimulating the eye and subtly extending the pallette. You should specify whether light, middle, or dark tones are required in your ordering of job lots.

Germany has specialised for some time in the production of opalescent antiques of great beauty.

29

16 *A crucible containing molten glass being taken from the furnace* (*Diderot*)

17 *A workman, wearing a protective mask, whirls the molten glass into the shape of a disc* (*Diderot*)

18 *Molten glass being shaped into cylinders, split, and flattened out into sheets* (*Diderot*)

These are flashed. The base colour is very much stronger than in normal flashed glass and the flash is a translucent whitish grey. Needless to say they look different whichever way round you hold them.

Texture of antique As well as colour and tone, the antique that is made today has a great deal of texture. This is to imitate the roughness and horniness and the irregularities and imperfections of the glass of the Middle Ages. It seldom succeeds in any kind of deception.

Bubbles are obtained by withdrawing the blowpipe from the 'pot' before the mixture of silica sand, borax, and colouring matter has boiled itself free of sulphurous gases formed in the heat of the chemical combination in the 'pot'. The longer the 'pot' brews, the cleaner and finer the glass comes out.

Striations occur only in French or German glass, and are made by the glass-blower who, when the bubble is the size of a rugby ball, twists and turns it in an iron bowl lined with small spikes, called a 'hedgehog' or 'porcupine'; this has the effect of streaking the glass with a fine, semi-regular network of striations which give French and German glass the brittle-looking crystalline structure of their surface, which glitters and glints in the sun. There is a more fluent hand-made version of this made in England known as streaky pot.

5 *Streaky or reamy glass* These are mostly English, though Germany makes some, called *Danziger Glas*.

Streaky, as its name implies, is a glass with irregular streaks in it, made by mixing two pots of glass together and stirring. It is nearly always flashed, but sometimes pot. It can be either of one colour, or of two or three colours together. All variations are made by the irregular banding and striping of the glass. They are of different thicknesses, and produce a strong degree of tonal contrast in the glass.

Reamy is a light variant of streaky. This glass was very much used by the stained glass masters earlier on in the century, who wanted to let a great deal of light into churches. The colours most often used are off-whites, yellows, greens, and light blues. It is remarkably easy to cut (which streaky is not), and is extremely susceptible to stain; but both Streaky and Reamy—one owing to the violence of its rhythms in the individual piece, the other owing to its generally weak tone, are not much used in modern stained glass. They both have the curiously historic or anachronistic flavour, of the days of the Art-Nouveau, and the Arts and Crafts Movement.

6 *Sanded glass* Occasionally sheets of antique are annealed on iron tables, which have been lightly spread over with grains of sand; the sand indents the glass, providing an all-over random texture.

7 *Curious* If you look around a wholesale warehouse which deals in glass, you will find various sheets of antique glass which are mistakes or 'seconds', so far as the manufacturers are concerned; and these are likely to be named 'curious', and sold off quite cheaply. It is possible to buy them and use them in glass to very great effect, but it is also possible—and very much more likely—to bring them back to the studio and find them quite impossible to use in a window. They may look very beautiful in the sheet, but put them into a stained glass composition, and they stand out like a sore thumb. They might do very well for Tiffany-type lampshades, but that is not in my line.

8 *Commercial sheet*—white and opalescent glass —should not be neglected. Sometimes the very lack of texture and almost banal frontality of the colour can be used extremely well in combination with antique, particularly over a large area, where the reiteration of the texture of the antique might be too much; and where the actual pieces of glass need to be broader and larger in concept and extent than antique can supply.

Packing
The English, as a rule, are conscientious packers, but are apt to send their glass in untidy wire baskets; these are stuffed with straw, and are very messy to unpack.

The French send their glass in horrible old boxes made of poplar wood, which are very difficult to unpack. Much wrenching and flanging is needed. Inside the boxes they pack the glass extremely well with corrugated paper and cardboard, and they are scrupulously well labelled. In receiving glass from makers in France for the last twelve years, I have had few pieces broken.

The Germans, regrettably, are the worst of the lot. Their crates are massive and heavy, and well made—but inside, the glass is packed with little care, pieces of glass and straw being stuffed in indiscriminately. This is a pity, because the glass itself is of such good quality. I have always had a considerable amount of breakage with German glass. In the ten years since I have written this book I have had little cause to revise this opinion.

Unpacking
When the glass arrives it is advisable to unpack the pieces as soon as possible, to see what the colours look like. But the first thing to do, on delivery of the glass, before signing the delivery note for the driver, is to rock the crate quite vigorously to and fro, and listen for any nasty sounds of broken glass. If there is a really nasty sound, sign the note 'unexamined believed to be broken', and contact your insurance agent.

When the top of the crate has been removed and the straw packing taken out, care must be taken to see that the crate is standing firmly, and, if possible, leaning back against a wall, with a long piece of wood wedged along the front edge below the bottom of the case. This will make sure that the crate is firm and able to resist any alteration in the centre of balance. After unloading part of a crate, the weight of the remaining sheets frequently causes the crate to lose balance and fall over.

When the glass is unpacked, it is a good idea to check off each sheet with the invoice. Each colour should have an appropriate code number, and the code number of the colour should be written on the sheet of glass. The coding should be compared, on the invoice and the sheets; and the sheets should add up to the exact amount of square-footage ordered.

Put all the different colours and numbers in separate upright piles around the studio, preferably not against the racks, as this will impede the putting away of the glass. Place strawboard or a little straw, or an appropriately sized piece of polystyrene on the floor, to set the glass on, otherwise you will get flakings or cracks starting when the glass—which is very delicate—hits the floor.

Make sure the colours are separate, the flashed colours and the pot colours kept apart. Ideally, when the colours are finally put in the racks, there should be a rack for each colour. This is not often possible: if you double up on a rack, with two colours, make sure that very contrasting colours are put together so that there will be no question of the two being confused. They should lean on the side of the rack.

Once the glass is put away, or as it is being put away, a sample should be cut and marked with the code number of the glass. Cut a fairly large piece; divide it into three. Put one in the chart at the end of the colour rack, one in the sample box, and one in a spare sample box. Often, when re-ordering, it is essential to send a sample of the colour you are talking about, and these samples can be mislaid or broken in the post, or mislaid at the glass factory: consequently I have always found a spare sample a great help.

Colour chart

Samples of glass (say 25 mm × 75 mm (1 in. × 3 in.)) can either be leaded up like a miniature window, or they can be slipped into a wooden frame with a small slip of calme in between; the frame is made so that the pieces of glass can be slipped out of the top, as occasion demands.

However, the best and simplest way is to arrange all the samples on a piece of plate glass, in the order of the glass racks; they are then waxed up or, better still, fixed with plasticine, so that they are easily removable and interchangeable. The only thing to watch here is that the glass rack number, as well as being *on* the glass, is engraved *below* the sample, on the plain glass also.

Note When the glass is unpacked and put round the studio prior to storing in the racks, it is important to keep the glass in roughly the same sizes —as often there are half-sheets, or broken sheets in the crates. Make sure the largest pieces, in the individual piles, are to the rear, and the smaller pieces progressively to the front. Keep the glass as near to upright as is practicable. Glass at 45° has every chance of sliding out at the bottom. When handling the new sheets of glass, inspect them closely for starts in the corners and elsewhere; a start, or small crack, can be extremely dangerous either in the handling of the sheet or in the racks. If you find a sheet with a start, either cut it across so as to break off the offending part; or else break the sheet along the start and divide it into two, so that the sheet is no longer a danger.

19 *Papier collé by John Piper* 1966

Cartooning and Designing

The cartoon, or working drawing, together with the cutline, are the vital link between the idea of the stained glass as conceived in sketches, and colour experiments and individual drawings, and the actual stained glass which is an amplification of the original idea contained in the sketch.

It is most important to see the cartoon in this light. Generally speaking, the cartoon should be of very little interest in its own right. If the sketch or the cartoon is too carefully worked out, the chances are that the resultant window will merely be a copy of the sketch made large, or a copy of the cartoon. I believe that you can only make one work of art once—come to one climax —and it is a mistake to think that the most important stage of the making of a stained glass window is in the cartoon. It is complete idiocy to think that it is contained in the sketch. I feel it is better to have a defective cartoon that leaves some leeway for spontaneity and imagination in the executing of the idea in glass, than to have a perfect cartoon rather pedestrianly and mechanically copied into glass.

The days of the carefully worked up cartoon in charcoal, with all the lead lines marked in, in double pencil, and the spaces between the charcoal stumping tastefully tinted—the whole being 'crispened' up by a little delicate pen-work— went out with the Pre-Raphaelites.

The days of the so-called perfect cartoon were the days of the Victorian system of apprentice-ship, when firms which boasted of turning out 'a window a day and two on Sunday', were dominated by the specialisation of stained glass, the cast-iron system of apprenticeship, and the growth of a genre of stained glass worker known as the 'painter'. In delegating every nuance of expression in a window to the 'painter'—who was not himself an artist, but was only a painstaking copyist—it was essential that the artist left no place for spontaneity; since everything artistic had to be delegated, the lines of delegation had to be made as scrupulous and watertight as possible.

Nowadays, with very much smaller stained glass establishments, where it is rare to find a man in charge who has not been to an art school and learnt first-hand what it is to design and draw and paint, the question of carefully worked-out cartoons hardly arises. Yet the nagging worry of being summary and slip-shod over a cartoon still persists.

In Germany, particularly in the tradition of Campendonk Thornprikker and Wendling, there is no nagging worry at all. In general the German tradition is brilliantly (and successfully) graphic and linear. All the artistic statement goes into the cartoon stage, and for anyone who has been lucky enough to see a full-scale cartoon straight from the hands of Ludwig Schaffrath, it is evident that such a cartoon is a supreme work of art in its own right. To a millimetre there is not one passage left unresolved or ambiguous over the whole cartoon.

This rigorous definition is carried out at no sacrifice of extreme delicacy of execution. The almost exclusive emphasis on line *for its own sake*, as opposed to line (as in Matisse's drawing) being a definition *between* spaces, means that the cartoon can and should be entirely unambiguous. It also means that, as a result, colour in German glass is used as an instrument of power as opposed to an instrument of feeling. Line, particularly subsidiary line, is used as an instrument of feeling—not unlike the use of decorations in Mozart's *Rondo in A*—'decorations' which convey so much emotion.

Though it is consciously intended and of the highest integrity Ludwig Schaffrath's mode of cartooning is at the same time highly appropriate for total delegation in the actual making of the glass. It is complementary to the almost Victorian system in Dr Oidtmann's studio where different craftsmen have been assisting their special artists in an unbroken personal tradition of some twenty-five years.

This is not unlike the great stained-glass firms of the nineteenth century in England, and quite parallel to the large stained glass firms in America—except that I see no evidence so far that large firms either English or American are employing artists of the extraordinary calibre of the great German designers of the fifties, sixties and seventies, whose work is slowly becoming known and being given its due.

There are two systems which I recommend as being most useful and most validly artistic in cartooning.

One is a scrupulously measured drawing, with the main shapes and rhythms precisely fixed—a full-sized cartoon, from which the full-sized cut-line can be drawn, if necessary, by someone else, though I always draw my own. The actual character of the paintwork and the choice of glass, and the exact harmony of colour, is left to the working on the glass in the studio window. If you are quite certain of your use of colour, the most economic way of working is straight from this outline cartoon in ink or charcoal. Placing, interval, and proportion are important in the cartoon; the rest can be put in as felt necessary.

The other method is to make a complete full-scale painting—water-colour, gouache, or oil—on paper for the whole window. The painting of a cartoon in colour means that the composition and placing of the emphasis of colour can be rapidly changed at will. Experimental syncopations of form, line, and colour, can be tried in a painted cartoon, provided what is basically feasible in glass is kept in mind, far more easily than working directly on the glass from a skeleton cartoon. Full coloured cartoons are very helpful in Gothic taceried windows.

Since the historic month of June 1975 taken by Ludwig Schaffrath at Burleighfield I have had good reason to add another and very important method of cartooning. This consists of two stages. The first stage is to make, preferably on cartridge paper that is squared (to inches or centimetres) an exact drawing in pencil of the proposed composition. Then make a full-scale cartoon on good paper. Square the paper to correspond to the original small cartoon's squares and sketch in lightly in charcoal the main lines. Then using more and more pressure on the charcoal, which should be broad willow (scene-painters) charcoal, get greater and progressively greater definition and authority in the cartoon. Main changes are easily elected during the preliminary strokes of the charcoal. When the cartoon is fully defined and authoritative, the charcoal lines should be fixed with a good fixative.

This method of cartooning by line only is imperative if you wish to continue the composition using the modern German method of glazing which consists of running two lead lines together so they meet and mutually turn, running parallel to one another producing together a lead line two, or sometimes three times as thick as a single lead. (See page 109 in the chapter on glazing for the effect of German cartooning on the design of German leadwork.)

The colour is usually indicated on these kind of cartoons only by means of coloured crayons or oil-pastels. Really emotional expression of colour is hardly ever attempted. It would in any case hardly coalesce with the vigorous line-expression.

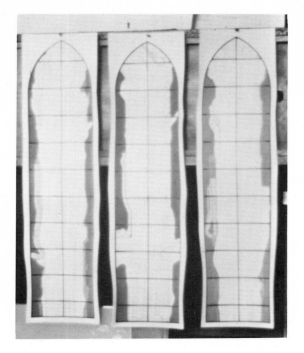

20 *Cartoons and sketches for St Joseph's Aachen,
photographed in the studio of Ludwig Schaffrath*

There are two things to remember about full-scale colour cartoons.

The first is that a cartoon is not to be slavishly copied into glass; the mental process in dealing with a colour cartoon is quite different from dealing with a skeleton cartoon. With a colour cartoon, the stained glass artist has to go back in mental chronology, and re-edit from the beginning a window that, mentally, is a *parallel achievement* to the cartoon. This is very much easier to do with another artist's cartoon than one's own, for the simple reason that in interpreting someone else's cartoon, only one mental journey is done. In interpreting one's own cartoon, a kind of parallel journey is made with the mental progress already expended on the colour cartoon.

Secondly, in cartooning in colour, it must always be remembered that emotional equivalents in colour that are valid in painting are, in many respects, quite different in stained glass—a particular passage of, say, blue and green dominated by a strong yellow in painting, if directly translated into glass, becomes a yellowish area dominated by blue. Blue becomes more vivid, red becomes more sombre or claustrophobic. Black passages, or large black lines, although sometimes effective, at other times tend to become mere negative areas between areas of light; so that a passage in a painted cartoon which is of colour strongly over-barred by black for dramatic effect may become, in glass, a series of disconnected, isolated emphases and patches of colour floating about in the void.

All isolated white passages in cartoons should be interpreted on the cutline with a smaller perimeter of lead—lessening the area, especially if the glass is unpainted, owing to the white's tendency to halate or spread.

When black passages are wanted in glass, the equivalent emotion-trigger must be found in very dark green, brown, or purple. What is used, in fact, is the emotional effect of black, but the means to get it are in the language of light, the language of stained glass—not the language of non-light, i.e. total obscurity, which is negative.

These are only a few of the *aperçus* that the stained glass artist will pick up in the course of years of work. Each individual will find out his own language.

Photographic cartoons
There has been an increasing use in recent years of photographic cartoons. The original sketch is blown up photographically to the right size of the cartoon. The photograph is then worked on in Indian ink, coloured perhaps, and serves as a basis to the cutline.

Superficially, this method has practically everything to commend it; but when it is examined, it does not really hold water. The objections are:

1 It is expensive.
2 It tends to distortion; using the best possible equipment there are always bound to be some distorted outlines and passages towards the periphery of the cartoon, however carefully the

photographic work is done. This is less noticeable in small-scale work than in large-scale cartoons; but it is precisely the problems of large-scale cartooning to which photographic cartooning seems to be the answer.

I have found that the individual pieces of photo-enlarging are, each of them, slightly distorted; and this leads, when they are put together, to a very serious amount of distortion, which is corrected only with a very great deal of labour.

3 As well as exaggerating the good points of a sketch (which may look excellent as a sketch) it exaggerates the pitfalls, too. Mistakes of emphasis in the sketch are ludicrously exaggerated, and most of the time spent on a photographic cartoon is time spent correcting the passages that appear to have gone wrong. Thus, the activity of manual cartooning, instead of being a positive statement on a large scale by the artist, with all its faults and drawbacks, is a negative one, because of all the correction that has to be done to the photographs.

Added to this, a photographic cartoon always gives the impression of being a *small* thing that has, by some devious inflated means, illegitimately become large. Through some subtle means of cross-reference in the sub-conscious, it does not look right to be quite so big.

Cartoons should be drawn on reasonable quality cartridge paper, with a border of about 50 mm (2 in.) all round, so that the cutline cloth can be pinned on to the cartoon without the drawing pins getting in the way of rulers and pencils during cut-lining.

It helps both technically and artistically to make the cartoon the *exact* size of the finished window.

It helps to have the saddle-bars and the division-bars marked in the cartoon. Not only will they have to be reckoned with when the glass is finally made, so that if their place is not allowed for they may occur at most inconvenient places, but the fact of having cross-bars through the cartoons gives the whole composition a grid or framework which can act as a very useful system of interval and reference, and helps to give firmness and strength to the design.

When to stop There comes a moment in the cartooning when any more than can be said at this stage transforms the cartoon into a more important artistic statement than the glass. In my opinion this is the time to stop cartooning. The final artistic statement in stained glass must come from working in the medium—in cutting, painting, and leading.

21 *Detail of cartoon by Jacques Villon for the windows at Metz Cathedral*

22 *Window designed by Ludwig Scaffrath, Heilbron, Germany*

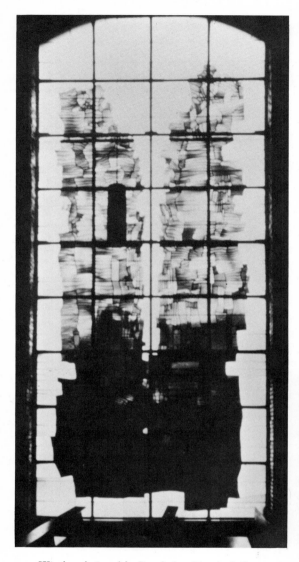

in giving concrete form to a tightly predetermined system of logical coherence. Most architects and many clients tend to like tight and precise sketches submitted to them. This does not work out well from an artist's point of view, since the vision is always evolving towards the finished product. In glass, the evolution is ended in the window. In architecture, more often than not, the evolution is ended in the plans and drawings. Some architects understand the artist's way of aiming at a definition, others are not so receptive.

Occasionally, especially in Germany and sometimes in America, by some miracle the artist fully understands the requirements of the architect and can produce a work of art that successfully combines the dynamism of a kind of technological aesthetic with the lyricism and spontaneity of the artist. In a word they combine the two seemingly impossible modes of thought, and when this happens in the hands of a real artist the result is a series of masterpieces.

23 Window designed by Buschulte, Siersdorf, Germany

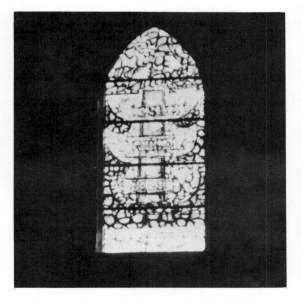

24 Jesse window in the Old Parish Church, Varengeville, Normandy, France. The last window that Georges Braque designed

Note The artistic method of thinking, and the architectural method of thinking, are completely different. Whereas the artistic mind works from vague generalities towards a uniquely defined statement, the architectural mind is occupied

Cutlines and Setting Up the Glass

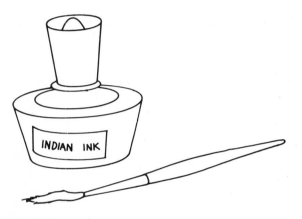

25 Cutlining equipment

The 'cutline' or tracing which is drawn over the cartoon is the only means of translating the cartoon into stained glass. It is well worth taking care over this because an accurate and well-designed cutline not only makes subsequent glazing extremely easy, even enjoyable, but also the necessity of having a cutline over the designed cartoon can be turned to advantage. Quite often the disposal of strong horizontal lines, and the division of a passage of the cartoon by means of lines which—though they may not necessarily follow the main lines of the design—are expressive in themselves, are an added counterpoint to the scheme of colour and areas of tonal contrast in the window.

I do not want to go into the aesthetic factors involved in the design of cutlines: there are as many ways of designing a cutline as there are of designing stained glass, and every individual has his particular peculiarities, but there are three faults which it would be better to avoid:

1 Archaising of any sort, which is very easy for a student to do, particularly if he takes medieval models to base his style on.
2 Slavish following of the cartoon, if this is designed in a very free way. If the design is greatly influenced by what could be called the painter's approach, it can sometimes very easily become extremely diffuse.
3 The over-rigid treatment of cutlines, which impose their character in a brutal way on the design and sometimes flatten and vulgarise the most sensitive of ideas in the cartoon stage. Usually students who are strongly linear by inclination, tend to clamp a very firm and definitive cutline like a strait-jacket on to a cartoon—or even work the cartoon up from the beginning with only the cutline in mind.

When all is said and done, the lead-line, of which the thin black line on the cutline cloth represents the heart, is drawn where the colour of the cartoon changes, and a new piece of glass is necessary. There are exceptions, but this is the main rule, and the closer it is stuck to the better.

Setting out the cutline

The cutline is traced over the cartoon either on

tracing-paper or on cutline cloth. Cutline cloth is now practically impossible to obtain because its general use in engineering blue-prints has been discontinued in favour of a kind of plastic sheeting which is of little use to the stained glass artist. However, I shall describe the cloth in case you are lucky enough to obtain it. Cutline cloth, or tracing cloth, or tracing linen, is very much more expensive than tracing paper but has certain distinct advantages. It does not tear; it does not disintegrate on the glazier's bench; if accidentally it gets wet, it still holds its shape to a large degree; it never disintegrates on the cutting-bench whilst you are cutting, and it is very easy to roll up and store away, and unroll at a moment's notice; it keeps its shape and flexibility for many years, which is important, because at some future time the window may have to be re-glazed, and then the original cutlines are invaluable. (I usually send the cutlines, suitably labelled, to the diocesan archives.)

There are various grades of tracing cloth—the cheapest about half as expensive as the dearest. For cutlines over black and white cartoons, where the division between the pieces of glass is fairly obvious, the cheaper sort of tracing cloth is quite good enough. For cutlining over coloured cartoons, where there are many dark or obscure passages, or where, if they have been designed by a painter, there is, for instance, some subtle edge value or outline that is important, the more expensive, finer-grained, and more transparent tracing cloth is the better.

If you use tracing cloth, the first thing to do, once you have unwrapped and unrolled it, and cut it off to the right length (having taken care to select the size of roll that is most apt for the width of the stained glass) is to tear off both side edges to within half an inch of the ruled line the whole length of the tracing cloth. This is to stop the tracing cloth from cockling at the edges, which it would do if you left it, thus distorting the cutline over the cartoon.

Mark out the perimeter of the panel or light, and make sure while you are about it that the measurements are the *sight* size of the stained glass, not the *full* size, because the cutline is only

for the cutting of the *glass* to the right size, not for the final fitting of the window.

You will notice that the cutline is dull on one side and glossy on the other. The dull side takes ink and pencil more easily than the glossy, so it is better to place the cutline on the cartoon *glossy side down*.

When you mark out the perimeter, make sure that you start with a good straight line the whole length of the light. Ex-WD (government) stock straight-edges are ideal for this, though they are difficult to obtain and expensive.

It is advisable to mark on the cutline the sight-width of the mullions if it is a mullioned window you are dealing with—and to make a note of the tracery in relation to the lights and to each other. It is always as well to check beforehand the sizes you have been given, making sure whether the length given is the total measurement of the height or only the length from the window cill to the springline (usually the base line of the cardboard template for the head of the light).

The corners of the panel must be marked out on the cutline perfectly square, and the measurements must be checked and made perfectly correct. 'Near enough' will not do as a measurement. It is either right or it is wrong: there is never an in-between stage. If you are using a template, for the head of a light or for tracery, for heaven's sake draw round it accurately, true to the actual shape of the template. It is best to draw both the division lines and the perimeter lines on the cutline in some other colour than pencil, from the actual architect's measurements given on the latest dated architect's drawing. It is advisable to do this direct from the architect's drawings and not from the cartoon you have drawn, as this will tend to avoid inaccuracy. If cut out sizes have been supplied to you it is as well to check the templates on the cut line as well.

Once this is done, the cutline is placed over the cartoon, either vertically attached to the wall, or on a table or bench, depending usually on whether the cartoon is in black-and-white or in colour. Trace lightly and fluently in not too soft a pencil (B or BB) all the main lines and shapes you wish to lead out, and the changes of colour that occur in the cartoon. As has been said at the beginning of the chapter, the cutlines play an extremely important part in the artistic expression of a window, but they are also a structural device to enable the pieces of glass to stay together when they are upright in the window. An element of balance and engineering and above all a sense of interval go towards contributing to the character of a good cutline; when these factors are lacking the resultant window may look rather flabby and unsatisfactory.

It is a good idea, having completed the pencilled cutline, to detach it from the cartoon and judge its main shapes and rhythms on their own: in many cases stained glass artists neglect the external effect of the window, which is an architectural factor of importance, and this is the right time to consider this part of the work. If there are any obviously bad shapes, they must be dealt with now, before the cutline is inked in.

If the glass is for a Gothic church, or has a shaped top, or if it is being made to be fixed into stonework or masonry, it will have to be made in sections, dividing the light into a series of panels. These may be of any size convenient for handling, and proportional to the character of the window, but the permanently fixed place for division is at the *spring-line*, at the top, where the segment of the curve closing the head of the light springs from (hence the term spring-line). A division must be made at this point; largely to help the fixers insert the head of the window in the masonry. If it is inconvenient to have it at this exact height, the spring-line can be moved up or down an inch or so, to accommodate a detail of the design, for instance, or to appear in harmony and proportion with the intervals chosen for the other division-bars; the eye will tolerate such a small discrepancy. Most stained glass lights, if longer than 60 cm (2 ft), are divided into sections, as has been mentioned above, because it simply is not practical to install stained glass all in one piece. The section lines are placed in proportion to the design and the size of the window. It is quite permissible to have them either all regularly spaced or progressively diminishing towards the top, or entirely regular, except the bottom division-

26 *Method of doing tracery lights on the Reyntiens' system*

bar which is sometimes higher than the rest, making the bottom section longer in proportion, than the sections above it.

Where the window opening is highly irregular —or where the design of the window itself is on the random side, you can indeed stagger the bar-lines so that they do not line through from light to light. I have even used a combination of fixed interval division bar-lines and random saddle bar lines (in the middle of the panel: see below). Occasionally when the design of the window allows it, the saddle bars can be canted from the horizontal as well. I think I used staggered and inclined bar lines to good effect in the porch window (Churchill Window) of Washington Cathedral, Washington DC. Between the division-bars, depending on the depth of the section, there are one or more bracing bars, known as saddle-bars, placed across the window-space; as the leads have to be tied to these and it is inadvisable to fix the ties on to the side of the lead calmes, extra lead is inserted cutting across the design, to mark the horizontal place where the saddle-bar will be, and to give two or more junctures of lead and solder, to which the copper-ties can be soldered in due time. The position of the saddle-bars should be indicated in the cartoon, and small horizontal lines where the saddle bars are proposed should be drawn on the cutline.

Where there is a division, you must of course allow for it in the cutlines.

A division-lead, which is fully described on pages 123–4, will take up 5 mm ($\frac{3}{16}$ in.) space between each of the sections; therefore rule two lines, 5 mm ($\frac{3}{16}$ in.) apart, wherever a division occurs.

The whole cutline, excluding the division-lines (in coloured ink) and the perimeter (in coloured ink or in pencil) should now be drawn in definitely with Indian ink. The best thing to use for the job is a fine, 12 mm ($\frac{1}{2}$ in.)-long camel-hair brush, such as signwriters use, dipped into the ink which is best poured out into an old-fashioned grand-piano-leg-wheel-stand made of glass. You can pick these up for next to nothing in any junk shop and they are practically unspillable, as well as holding just the right amount of ink to refill your brush. The line should never be more than 2 mm ($\frac{1}{16}$ in.) wide; with a brush it is possible to get that much more fluency of line which gives a decision and character to the cutline.

The 2 mm ($\frac{1}{16}$ in.) line in ink must be kept entirely regular and even (and to do this, ink-cutlining is best done on a broad table, horizontally), because the 2 mm ($\frac{1}{16}$ in.) thickness of the line represents the heart of the lead you will use in glazing, and if the glass is cut with less or more than that space between it and its neighbour, you will find that it will be impossible to glaze it accurately —so that a fault in the cutlining only comes to light at the very end of the process of stained glass, when it is too late to take any but the most drastic action, involving perhaps the mutilation of the original design.

If the lines on the cutline are intended to be straight, then make them really straight; a straight-edge must be used for drawing them, and when subsequently using ink it is best to make use of a bridge. A bridge is a piece of wood, usually 38 mm × 19 mm ($1\frac{1}{2}$ in. × $\frac{3}{4}$ in.) section, horizontally (with the flatter face up) attached to two smaller blocks of wood fastened at either end: the little blocks can stand proud either side of the

horizontal piece of wood (being about 50–57 mm (2–2$\frac{1}{4}$ in.) long themselves) to ensure stability. Since the hand has to run smoothly along the length of wood when making ink-lines, the better finished the surface and the rounder and smoother the corners of the wood, the better.

When making curves or wobbly lines it is best to exaggerate them slightly, as they will tend to lose their character or shape in the process of leading up. Cutlined curves inevitably tend to flatten out during the actual process of leading up.

Now is the time to inspect the completed cutline, and note if it contains any glaring faults of technique, as opposed to art.

Does the cutline mean that anyone using it will have to cut impossible curves or shapes or re-entrant angles or pieces of glass so large or so small as to defy handling at a later stage? Sickle-shaped and wishbone-shaped and crescent-moon-shaped pieces are obvious worries which should be eliminated. Everything, in fact, that makes for idiocy, rather than difficulty, of technique.

The next job is to mark out the cutline on to an easel or a piece of plate glass. Lay the cutline down on a flat bench with the *reverse side uppermost*, if you are using the plate-glass method of viewing and painting the stained glass. Then lay your plate glass panel down on top of it squarely, making sure, if several pieces of plate glass are being used (as on the grid-type easel), that you allow the right gap between the individual pieces of plate glass. In the latter case it is a good plan to have the sections of plate glass coinciding with the size of the stained glass panel sections. The time saved and the extra convenience is well worth the expense of buying new glass the right size for a new job.

With the *wooden-bound* easel-type of stained glass mounting, the best way of attaching the cutline is by lifting up small wedged-shaped pieces of the cutline, having previously laid the cutline accurately, *face up*, on one side of the easel, which is horizontally laid on two benches. These wedge-shaped pieces are made by two convergent diagonal cuts with a razor-blade, and the resultant tongue of cutline cloth is lifted up, a spoonful of very hot wax is dished into the triangular hole, and the section of cutline cloth is folded back and pressed home onto the wax before it has time to go hard. Intervals of 60 or 90 cm (2 or 3 ft) are usually sufficient to make the cutline stick the whole length of the easel, which can then be reversed by two people and lead-lined on the back, following the *reversed* pattern on the cutline.

Lead-lining

Lead-lining is the drawing of black lines on the back of the plate glass which is holding the stained glass. As their name implies, the lines take the place of the lead and follow exactly the pattern of the cutline. With the lead-lines in position, it is possible to see to a large extent how the finished window is going to look. Without lead-lines, not only is it difficult to place, or replace, the individual pieces of stained glass, but owing to so much light coming through between these pieces, the true tonal and colour pattern of the window is not apparent, because the colour is given a false overall unity of effect by the white light all round it.

When the cutline is attached to the plate glass, or the plate glass is laid on the cutline, the lead-lining is traced on the other side of the glass.

Mix into a smooth paste a little vegetable black, or lamp-black, and water, together with a little gum arabic. It is important to get true vegetable black at an ironmonger's—'coloring black' for concrete, or black powder paint in so-called 'art' colours, are never as efficient—they do not flow so easily, and are apt to dry up in the middle of a brush stroke. Never attempt to use Indian ink in the lead-line black. Dilute the smooth paste you have made with sufficient water to 'set up' the black, but not enough to make it a flowing liquid. Use a 19 mm ($\frac{3}{4}$ in.) long, soft-haired, flowing brush of about 5 mm to 6mm ($\frac{3}{16}$ in. to $\frac{1}{4}$ in.) diameter ferrule. Try to keep the black paint only at the end of the brush. Paint the lines of the cutline evenly and accurately, and check that they are being painted *in reverse*. (It is very easy to make a mistake about this.) Make sure that the brush is directly over the cutline and that the black lines are an even 9 mm ($\frac{3}{8}$ in.) wide. If the lines of the cutline are closer

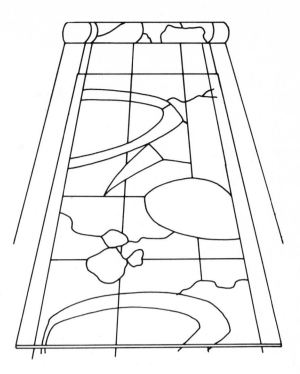

27 *The cutline laid out with clear glass on top*

together, then obviously it may be necessary to make the lines of the lead-lining narrower, so that you can at any rate see the coloured glass between.

Use another broader and thicker brush to put a 50 mm to 63 mm (2 in. to 2$\frac{1}{2}$ in.) border of black all round the perimeter of the lead-lining, and fill in any tracery or cusping solid with the black, unless it is going to be covered with a black paper mask. Leave the whole thing to dry. When it is dry, turn over the panel and on the clean side, wherever two lines of the lead-lining converge on a point, and where they meet the perimeter—at every junction in fact—press a small neat ball or blob of plasticine with your thumb. Do not tear the plasticine and stick it on haphazardly anyhow, roll it up neatly so the blob is round and rather less than 12 mm ($\frac{1}{2}$ in.) in diameter. This is so that, if the glass is accurately cut, it is easy to attach it to the plate glass without the pattern of the actual glass being distorted in relation to the cut-line or the lead-line.

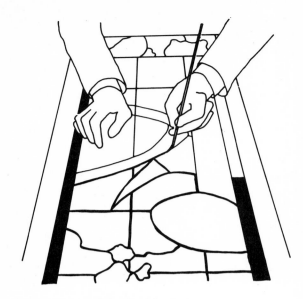

28 *Clear glass being lead-lined*

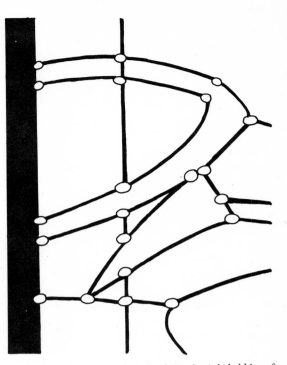

30 *Plate glass, having been lead-lined with bobbles of plasticine*

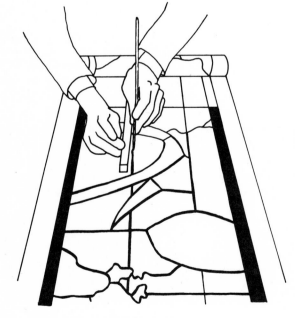

29 *Clear glass being lead-lined in straight lines using the bridge*

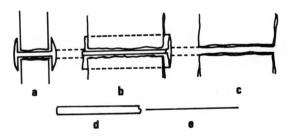

31 a *Cross section showing distance between glass being occupied by the heart of the calme*
   b *Same, as seen from above. Top leaf of lead removed*
   c *Distance of pieces of glass away from each other when laid on the cutline*
   d *Right width of cutline inked line. The glass is cut to the border of this line*
   e *Ineffectual cutline, too narrow*

Clean and polish each piece of antique glass before you press it on to the plasticine, and if there is going to be some time elapsing before working on the panel, cover up the whole thing so that it does not get dusty.

If you now erect your easel or panels of plate glass in order, you can see at once the whole ordered disposition of lead-line, glass and colour.

Another method of attaching glass to an easel is the older method of waxing. Using the wax-bath, melt up pure new beeswax (for the best adhesion) and spoon it between joints and on junctures, after having laid out the stained glass over the lead-lining on the other side of the plate glass which will have been *re*-reversed by this time. The wax must be really hot to stick the glass on—half heat will not do. The waxing of the glass *may* be done before the lead-lining, using the cutline (which has been attached by wax to the underside of the glass easel) as a guide for laying out the glass, then waxing the glass in position and afterwards lead-lining the glass on the easel, upright, or horizontally, laid on two trestles.

If there is a high degree of accuracy needed in the painting of the window, the last-mentioned method is, without doubt, the most accurate way of laying out glass. It was used throughout the nineteenth century for the great number of Gothic Revival windows made in England.

Continental method

In Germany and France, where they cut their glass in the marked template manner, the lead-lining is not done because there is no cutline to go by after the templates have been cut by double scissors. Instead of lead-lining and using easels and plate glass, the stained glass craftsman leads up the glass on the bench straight after it is cut, in very light lead, and only solders it on one side. The panels are then put up, painted, and torn apart, the glass to be fired, and the lead to be melted down again and made into fresh calmes. Not only does this system contribute to a greater inflexibility of technique, since the colour of the glass cannot be changed once it is set up, encased in lead, but it seems to be a logical extension of the

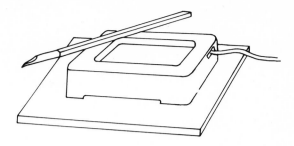

32 *Patent wax bath with copper dipper*

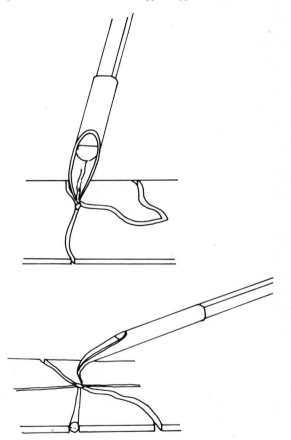

33 *Method of spooning in wax waxing the glass*

greater use on the Continent of lead-melting and calme-milling within the regime of the studio. Since the English now buy their lead calmes from manufacturers, they are reluctant to put their lead bills up more than they have to, only getting a discount for scrap.

Cutting Glass

The cutting bench

The cutting bench should be at a comfortable height—a little higher than an ordinary table, on the level of the lower ribs, so that it is possible to lean over it. Though the glass on which the cutting is done can be level, it is best set at a slight angle from back to front.

Obviously in the template method of cutting the use of light tables or benches and portable light-boxes is beside the point. If you wish to use the template method, the next six paragraphs can be ignored.

Permanent cutting bench

A permanent immovable cutting bench can be in the form of a light-box. A long piece of glass forms the top, the three sides being boxed in with plywood or hardboard, and the fourth side open to the natural daylight, which is reflected upwards by a large mirror placed inside the box at an angle of 45° to catch the light at the end of the studio. The glass top should be large enough to take the working area when you are cutting, the tray at the side which receives the cut pieces in order, and the tools and the many odd pieces of glass that are lying around during the process of cutting. The glass should be 6 mm ($\frac{1}{4}$ in.) plate in all cutting tables or boxes.

The permanent light-box, alternatively, can be lit entirely by electric light. The inside of the light-box is painted white and there is no mirror. Such a light-box is a permanent structure; it is heavy and often gets in the way in the main studio. It can be put on castors to make it easier to put out of the way, but it is useless when the cutting is not being done, and two such light-tables in the studio are a waste of space.

Portable light-box

Unless there is room in the whole studio complex for a separate room for cutting, which has disadvantages in any case, the best apparatus for cutting is a simple portable light-box.

The advantages of this are that it is compact, and two or three can be kept in the studio at a time, hanging on pegs on the wall or on shelves, and taken down when they are needed.

The box is easily made at home. All that is needed is a square frame, on short legs if possible, and a small rebate let in along the perimeter at the top, so that a slab of 6 mm ($\frac{1}{4}$ in.) plate glass about 60 cm sq (2 ft sq) can be let into the top. Previous to this, an ordinary electric lamp fitting should be screwed to the further, higher side of the light-box. The electric bulb should not be so close to the plate glass as to radiate enough heat to crack the plate glass in the course of a day's session of cutting. There should be a bright tin reflector lining the base of the portable light-box, but this should not be permanently fixed as chips of glass and dust should be removed from the light-box occasionally. There can also be fixed to the light-box a system of clips or pins of wire to hold the cutline securely and prevent it slipping off whilst you are working—a very common occurrence— though if you are working all over the cutline,

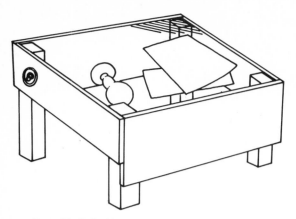

34 *Portable light-box*

i.e. on a series of blues up and down the window, this immobility of the cutline can become a nuisance.

When needed for cutting, put the light-box on the studio table or bench, close to the supply of large sheets of glass. The short legs should bring the height of the cutting surface to just under chest height. Isolate it from the rest of the table on which it is standing, as this prevents any accumulation of glass bits and pieces round the actual area of cutting, enabling the cutline to be moved freely to and fro without sending a shower of glass on to the floor. At the same time, the table or bench on which the cutting box is placed should be large enough, like the light-box, to hold the tray which receives the cut pieces and the odd pieces of glass themselves. In the case of plate glass alone being used, you must have room to lay the *plate-glass* panel flat down on the table, instead of a tray, so that you can clean the cut glass and press it straight down on to the plasticine blobs. Right beside the cutting box, half slipped under the table or bench, it is as well to have the waste bin or waste box, on wheels. This should be at the right height to be able to slip under the table on its wheeled base. The height of the rim will be found to be the ideal height to jettison small pieces of glass accurately into the waste bin. This action, like so much of the mechanical drudgery of stained glass, becomes a reflex action. The alternative to using the waste bin is (a) to leave pieces of unwanted glass and chips of glass

on the bench; or (b) to scatter them around you on the floor—and either course of action is unsatisfactory, for obvious reasons.

When cutting it is always as well to stand on a duck-board. A duck-board is a small section of wooden flooring about 50 mm × 76 mm (2 in. × 3 in.) made of horizontal slats nailed onto a cross-base of wood. It prevents one's shoes being in direct contact with the floor. This is warmer in winter, and cooler in summer, and less tiring on the feet should the floor of the studio be concrete. It does of course prevent pieces of glass coming into contact with one's shoes.

Continental method of cutting

In this book the English method of cutting and cutline procedure is described. Having used the French and German method, as well as the English, I find that the advantages and disadvantages of each are complementary; that is, the Continental method of cutting and glazing is extremely efficient, quick, clean, and economical, and it enables the windows to be produced at a lower price-range; but—and it is a significant but—it does not necessarily help the window to become a work of art, because the method is too mechanical and inflexible for sudden changes or improvements to be made in the course of preparation.

German tools

Before the glazing techniques of the continent are discussed, a word would be appropriate on the 'philosophy of tools'. Man, it has been said, is a tool-making animal: and on this count the Germans must be very manly indeed. There is an inconceivable profusion of tools in Germany for stained glass, especially where glazing is concerned.

I do not think having a large number of tools is a good idea. In fact the fewer the better. The reason is simple—the less tools you have the more versatile and resourceful your hand and brain must be. Reliance on masses of rather too specialised tools is, in my view, an indication of an inner identity crises. Perhaps this is fanciful—and the German achievement in glazing is proof itself of the goodness of having specialised equipment.

47

Laying out
Metal rules

In Germany it is usual to use well bevelled metal rules as a base from which to glaze. These give a very beautiful and perfect edge to the panel and are well worth using.

Cutting lead

The German method is to use the sickle-shaped knife in a rocking forward, guillotining action. It is more suitable with softer lead.

Cutlining

The German method, being cut on shapes, can be glazed without a cutline and indeed, with the original cutline cut into a large number of little shapes, this is often obligatory, generally speaking.

Double cutlining

The Germans are adept at turning two leads to meet each other and run parallel, producing a lead image of double width and intensity. They also use the 'stop' in glazing, i.e. produce an effect of one large lead over-running a transverse lead and finishing 'in mid air' halfway across the glass. Not unlike the dextrous tricks of late fourteenth to fifteenth century vault ribs in South Germany and Bohemia which also 'cut off'.

These modes of expression degenerate very quickly into an irritating mannerism with nothing to express. They are comparatively easy to do in cutting the templates by means of double edged scissors.

Wooden battens

The English method is usually to use wooden battens to define the area to be glazed. This does have disadvantages in that the wood *can* warp with the consequence that the panel looks distorted. But one marvellous advantage is that you can use the batten (next to you) as a block on which to cut the lead.

The English method is to cut directly downwards with a square knife. The practice of 'vibration' is possible using this method but it is impossible using the German method.

English method is *not* as succinct and smooth as the German method. On the other hand it *can* be used in a more flexible way, i.e. one can improvise glazing as one goes along.

Not using the double edged scissors the double cutline method is virtually impossible in England. The mannerisms associated with this clever technique are thus avoided.

Tools
(a) Diamond cutter
(b) Steel-wheel cutter
(c) Tapper (for slab)
(d) Grozer
(e) Plate pliers of various sorts
(f) Small hand grindstone

Requisites for the maintenance of the tools:
Coarse and fine stones, oil
Then in addition you will need:
Template glass, whitening, carbon paper, a pounce bag, a good black pencil, a chinagraph or wax pencil, a rule.

(a) Diamond cutter

In the face of so many legends of initials and love sonnets being engraved on window-panes with diamonds in the past, it is disappointing to discover that the diamond is extremely limited in manœuvrability, and owing to this limitation is practically useless in stained glass, except for the cutting of straight lines. Since we don't want to change cutter every time the line changes from curved to straight, the stained glass cutter can quite well do without a diamond altogether. Diamonds are used in the trade for cutting plate—and commercial glass—and they are useful for this because they never wear out. But apart from their use in cutting quarries, either lozenge-shaped or square, they have little part in stained glass except in Germany, where they have very elegant diamond cutters, set in attractive wood handles, which are principally used for cutting absolutely opaque white antique pot-glass. This has the consistency, brittleness and hardness of porcelain and would inevitably not respond to a steel cutting wheel at all.

(b) Steel-wheel cutter

Without a doubt, the steel-wheel cutter is the best all-round instrument with which to cut antique and slab glass. It is as mobile as a one-wheeled cycle (which it resembles), and can be pushed along the glass or dragged down the glass, turned round sharp corners, do sweeping curves, as well as straight lines. It is very sensitive under the hand, and an experienced worker can execute anything he wants in the way of cutting, simply by careful manipulation.

The cutter consists of a cast-iron handle at the end of which the steel wheel is inserted on a tiny spindle. The serrations in the top part of the handle are grozing serrations and are useful for grozing off small pieces of glass, and for fine work in the inside of curves, or on delicate glass or tricky shapes in general.

The handle proper, which tapers at the end and has a broad pad just before the grozing slots, shaped rather like a cobra's hood, can be either true, i.e. in one axis with the cutting wheel, or can be set-off in a parallel axis.

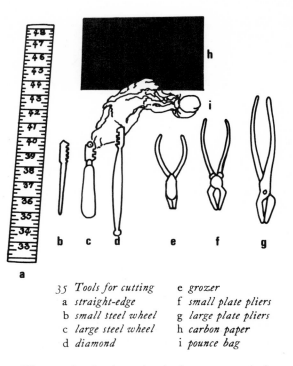

35 *Tools for cutting*
a *straight-edge* e *grozer*
b *small steel wheel* f *small plate pliers*
c *large steel wheel* g *large plate pliers*
d *diamond* h *carbon paper*
  i *pounce bag*

The steel wheel, a simple instrument, is by any account the best instrument to use, but as there are variations of it on the market, these should be noted and avoided.

Steel wheels to be avoided

(i) The large wooden-handled steel wheel with with a rotary end containing six substitute wheels, which can be turned round and used as the previous one becomes worn out. This is a heavy, cumbersome instrument—expensive, uncomfortable in the hand, and a false economy.

(ii) The tungsten wheel. The wheel part of this cutter, the handle of which is generally painted green in England, in distinction to the steel wheel's red, is too hard for the comparatively delicate task of cutting. Although it will hardly ever wear out, it will bruise the glass in cutting, and result in a coarse cut. Sometimes the tungsten wheel is fitted in to a soft-metal handle, so that the sleeve holding the sprocket is apt to wear out first, leaving a limping cutter.

(iii) The interchangeable steel cutter with a small clip device on the side, so that the wheel can slipped out and a new one inserted. This can be extremely useful provided that the wheel and clip really work as they are meant to. The clip usually works loose before the wheel is used up.

Every studio has, I suppose, its one extravagance, and mine is undoubtedly the liberal use of plain steel cutters. The feel of a good, light, new steel cutter under the hand is worth all the extra economy and bother of trying to cope with any other sort.

Sharpening the cutter
If the cutter does get generally blunt, it can be sharpened quite easily—though I do not like working with such sharpened instruments.

First remove the shoulders of the cutter by filing or grinding to lie back at an angle of 45° or so (diagram 37) then oil the cutter on the wheel and the spindle and, using a slate or an oilstone, hold the cutter as shown in the diagram running it up and down the slate or stone, taking great care to hold the wheel at the same angle all the time and not to pull it across the stone sideways as this will damage the cutting edge.

Spare wheels and spindles can be bought, and can be changed quite easily—there is nothing against this, unless the handle is made of some softer metal than iron, in which case it may well be a waste of time because the spindle of the wheel will wear away the socket of the holder and make the wheel impossible to control owing to its looseness.

(c) *The tapper* has two small brass balls either end of a 102 mm to 127 mm (4 in. to 5 in.) small steel pin; not much seen today—but useful for the tapping of cuts in Norman slabs, particularly the thick centre parts. I recommend that if you want one of these tools you should get one made specially for you. Old leather musical cases had a tiny kind of brass dumb-bell which flipped over a leather handle before you carried the case. I suggest that this type of brass dumb-bell is exactly what is required.

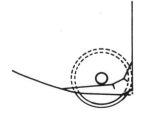

36 Tapper

(d) *The grozer* is made by the stained glass artist himself from a carefully ground-down small pair of pliers. It can be any size to suit himself, but is usually smaller rather than bigger because it is intended to be a more delicate instrument than the plate pliers. German grozers, as indeed German plate-pliers, are of the greatest delicacy and easy to use in the hand: like all German tools they are exceedingly well made.

(e) *Plate pliers*, after the cutter, are the most useful instrument of the cutting bench. Though one size—middle—is ample, it can be an advantage to have two or three sizes. The inside lip of the plate pliers is apt to wear down into a comfortable slope with time and use—but this should always be ground down and rectified. Plate pliers should always have a certain feeling of attack or bite on a piece of glass.

(f) *A small hand grindstone* is useful if it is attached to the side of the table. If any bumps or irregularities are too difficult for the grozer or plate pliers to deal with, the grindstone is extremely useful. It is also useful for grinding away sharp and prominent points and edges left on completion of the cutting of the glass—points and edges that can produce cuts on the hands, and cause your brushes and badger to lose more hairs than they otherwise would.

37 Method of sharpening a wheel

Cutting

When you start cutting, hold the cutter as shown in the diagrams. This will enable you to keep it straight, and give enough pressure where needed.

Many people hold the cutter in the same way as a pen, and wonder why they can never get a good cut, a reliable grip, and control over the cutter. Some people even hold the cutter with the wheel coming out of the bottom of their fist. The cutter should never be held like a linoleum-cutting knife. When making a cut, it should always be held at right angles to the glass (being a wheeled instrument the rules of conduct are remarkably like those of riding a bicycle). The cutter should more often than not be drawn towards you, and when following a curve, on cutline or on template, your wrist and elbow should be the guiding factor: the action should be a fluent one, involving the movement of the whole arm. Cutting is never concerned with the screwed-up action of the fingers alone. Think of the cutter as an extension of your pointing finger, and you will always get a good, continuous line. When cutting it is important to cut, never in jerks, but in a straight smooth line, a steady sweep of the hand.

Always, above all, be sure that your cutter is in first-class working condition. A good *cutter* glides smoothly across the glass without a hitch, and a good *cut* is practically invisible and merely heard during the process of cutting. Often, with very new cutters, the tendency is to press too hard, and especially if the glass is on the soft side, there is a trail of minute splinters scattering off either side, in the wake of the cut that has just been made. This is not a good cut.

If too much pressure is put on the cutter, the only result is that the glass gets scratched and damaged. If the cutter misses and goes off at a tangent across the glass, or if there is a break in the cut, and if this break is repeated at 19 mm ($\frac{3}{4}$ in.) intervals, you immediately know that you have got a flat on the wheel. In this case, discard the cutter or change the wheel. When cuts which have been made with a flat cutter are tapped, they invariably follow the cut as long as it is true, and then whizz off at a sudden diagonal when they meet the flat spot.

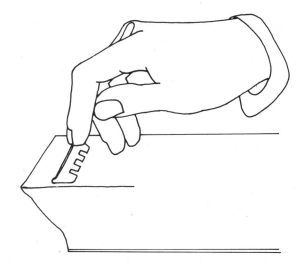

38 Holding the cutter

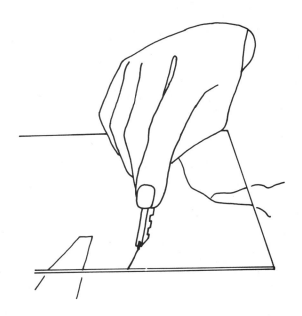

39 Holding the cutter, front view

51

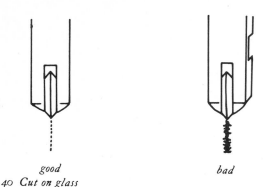

good   *bad*

40 *Cut on glass*

Cutting large pieces

If it is necessary to cut along the length or breadth of a large piece of glass with one smooth, clean cut, the best way to do this is with a fairly old cutter (running along a rule or a setsquare), with the piece of glass lying flat on the table. Insert the smallest part of the handle of the cutter under this score-mark at one end, and by using gentle pressure on each side of the handle the glass will split evenly right along the cut.

Another method of cutting large pieces of glass is to lay the cut along the rule (the rule being underneath) so that it is a fraction of an inch (5 mm) forward of the edge of the rule. The one half is kept firm with the right hand and the other is gently flanged down across the edge of the rule.

Another method is similar, using the edge of the table instead of the rule.

A further method for middle-sized pieces of glass is to hold the glass lightly in both hands (after having made the cut) and bring the knee up to the glass (not the other way round) quite gently and smoothly. The sheet will part quite easily into two. This is a technique which is unorthodox, but with a great deal of practice I have never known it fail.

Choice of glass

Generally speaking, the plainer and less interesting the glass is in itself, the more likely the window is to be a personal success. The use of figured or streaked glass in a window, particularly if it is for general purposes and not for a particular

passage, is exactly like the use of quotations in writing a book: too many can ruin original work. The artist is not using his own method of expression, but is relying on the picked-up secondhand expression of someone he has never seen or known, i.e. the glass-blower at the antique factory.

Temper of glass

Large pieces of glass have been annealed in the factory before coming into the stained glass studio.

Annealing is a haphazard process at the best of times. Basically, it consists of the glass being so slowly cooled that the molecular structure within

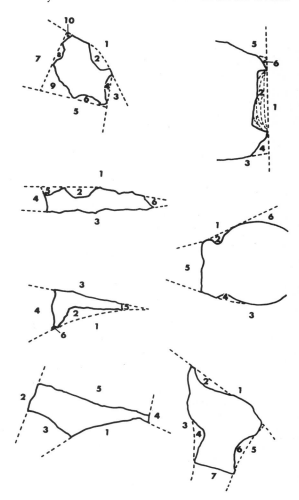

41 *Sequential method of cutting pieces of glass*

the glass has time to fit correctly together. If the annealing is too quick or inadequate, the resultant glass will be under permanent molecular tension. This fact is mentioned here because it is in handling the glass for cutting that you first become aware of the phenomenon and wonder how to cope with it.

English glass is the best tempered and therefore the best to cut.

French glass is reasonably well tempered, but the flashed glass is apt to fly the first time a cutter touches it.

German glass is invariably rather badly tempered, and will again fly at the first touch of a cutter.

The experienced stained glass worker will know from the feel and handle of his glass whether it is well annealed or not. Well-annealed glass has a safe, inert feeling about it. Badly annealed glass feels tense and nervous to the touch when handled in large sheets, and sometimes twitches and whips in the hands. But so long as the glass, however badly tempered, is handled gently but firmly no accidents are likely to occur, and no glass will be lost in the cutting.

Flashed glass

Generally speaking, flashed glass should be cut on the base-side, that is the thicker, white, side. Always shell a little glass from the edge of the piece with the grozing notches on your cutter, to see if it is flashed, and on which side it is flashed. If the piece of glass is small enough to be looked at sideways, a quick sideways examination will always tell you which side the flash is. Red flashed glass is impossible to cut on the flashed side anyway, because the red is far too hard. Green and blue flashed glass, though they are perfectly capable of being cut on the flash side, are better treated by being cut on the base-side; the cut on the flash, more often than not, bruises the flash layer, and does not penetrate further than the depth of the flash. This makes the act of completing the cut very hard work, and sometimes the cut is distorted considerably by the cut entering the base and going off, without guidance, at a tangent.

Medium-sized cutting

This category covers most of the day-to-day cutting that is done in stained class. The action of handling and using the cutter is identical to that described earlier on. The glass should be cut all round, in the order described in the cutting diagram on page 52. If this diagram is studied, it will be seen that the process is entirely logical. The pieces that one expects to be the first to come off do indeed do so, then the smaller pieces, and lastly any of the tricky passages.

The cut having been made with the cutter, it can be deepened by tapping on the underside with the nose or heel of the cutter, not with the steel wheel, which would cause a flat on the wheel immediately. The act of tapping is not nearly so aggresive an act against the glass as beginners think it has to be. The rift in the glass has already been started by the cutter, even though this may be practically invisible. All the tapping does is to lengthen and deepen an already existing fissure. Not much brute strength is needed for this, but a great deal of accuracy. If the tap by the cutter is not *exactly under* the fissure, nothing will result at all. Many beginners are exasperated by the inability of the glass to crack, not noticing that their taps are wildly wide of the mark. Once the habit of accurate tapping has been acquired, the act of cutting glass, which apparently is the most difficult thing for beginners to acquire, becomes easy and almost a reflex action, letting the mind dwell on what is really important, the selection of colour and tone. If the cut is tapped a little to one side or a little to another, the fissure will widen, but in the direction that the tap was given. Then, with slightly inaccurate taps, it is possible to get a wavy line on one side whilst having a constant straight line on the other side; this happens especially in thick glass or flashed glass.

Breaking

Either with tapping or without, the art of breaking glass is extremely simple. If you make a cut, and then hold the glass with both hands at the edge, with your thumbs on the top pressing down, and your first fingers right under the cut—if you press up with your fingers, the glass will break evenly along the length of the cut.

If you hold the glass in one hand, with the thumb of the other hand resting on the edge of the glass, the cutter resting on the fingers of the same hand with the heel pointing uppermost to the underside of the glass (the cut being on top), by working the hand holding the cutter and bringing the cutter up to the glass to tap it sharply but gently and accurately underneath the cut, the glass will break cleanly.

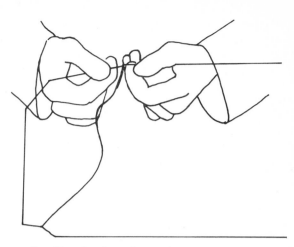

45 *Breaking the glass after cutting*

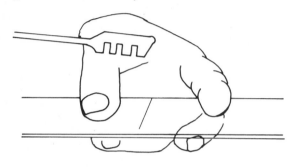

42 *Tapping the glass with cutter. The cutter is held in one hand and the glass held in the other*

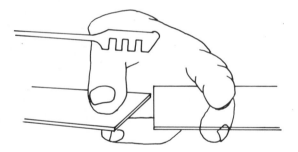

43 *Glass breaking in two but both pieces held by one hand*

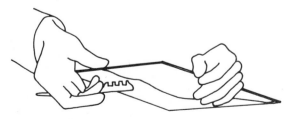

44 *Showing how to hold cutter whilst tapping a cut*

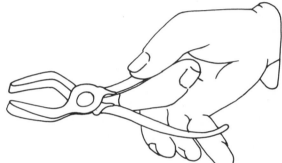

46 *Correct method of holding plate pliers in one hand*

1

2

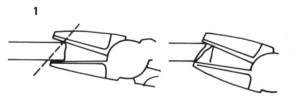
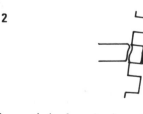

47 *Two methods of grozing in section*
    1 *plate pliers*
    2 *grozing teeth on cutter*

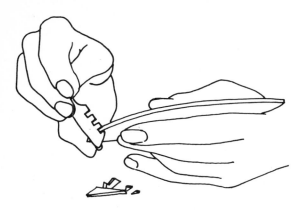

48 *Using the grozing teeth in cutting glass*

Cutting difficult shapes

When cutting more difficult shapes, it is necessary to tap the starting crack all along. If many little taps are given all along, the chances are that the two pieces will gently fall apart, or can be pulled gently apart in your fingers. If they do not fall apart, either the shape is too complicated or re-entrant, or the tapping has been done irregularly, as described in the previous paragraph. All tapping of shallow curves should be started from each end, and gently made to meet in the middle, so that the crack has least chance of running across the glass at a tangent.

When doing a tight curve, start at the apex of the curve and work outwards towards the edge of the glass in both directions; keep tapping until the glass works loose or falls out.

If the piece of glass that is not being held onto by the hand is allowed to fall, the cut may have been worthless. To stop this fairly common and irritating thing happening, the glass may be held in the left hand in the following way. Assuming the cut is marked on the glass, hold the piece of glass between the first (on top) and the second (on the bottom) fingers, *one* side of the cut; and between the thumb (on top) and the little or the third finger (on the bottom) on the other side of the cut. Your palm will be facing in towards yourself and the cut will be at right angles to the palm. In the course of tapping the shape out with the right hand, when the two pieces of glass finally fall apart, they will be still held, though

apart, in the grip of the left hand. This skill sounds difficult, but in fact it is a sleight of hand that comes easily with practice (see diagrams on page 54).

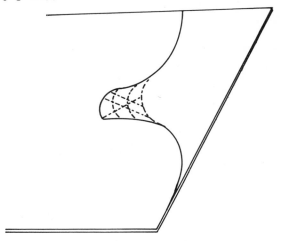

49 *Method of cutting difficult shapes*

It is always well to remember that in English cutting, when following the pattern of the cut-line, if you keep the outer edge of the cutter to the outside of the line you are following, the position of the wheel will be in just the right relationship to the cutline, and will leave enough room between the pieces of glass so cut, to accommodate the width of the heart of the lead when glazing.

In the Continental method, all permanent cut-line cloths are eliminated and are not subsequently used for leading-up. Instead, a piece of stout tracing paper is superimposed on the cartoon, and on this the cutline is traced. (There may be times when the cutline paper is duplicated, subsequently to be used in glazing, but this is rare). Having made the decision as to what colour is going to be used and where, in the abstract, without reference to the coloured glass except through samples, the code number of the panel and the code number of the glass is marked on the compartment of the tracing paper that corresponds to the glass to be cut.

The whole cutline is then divided by means of a two-bladed pair of scissors or a two-bladed knife (i.e. a Stanley knife used double, with a space between the blades)—the width between the blades corresponding to the width of the heart of the lead to be used. The fine filigree of paper resulting is thrown away, and the pieces of paper left over are used as templates from which to cut the glass. It is possible, in a large commission, to delegate to several cutters a pile of templates—a pile of reds to A, a pile of greens to B, a pile of blues to C, and so on. All the work gets done and the glass is cut, but with no visual reference between colours. Highly efficient, but not integral; it is not the logical way the artist works in building up an image and making a statement. However, on very large commissions, it is a useful method to know of, and be prepared for.

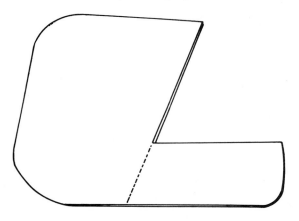

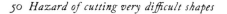
50 Hazard of cutting very difficult shapes

Extra-difficult cutting
Insertion is the placing of one piece of glass in the middle of an unbroken area of glass.

To cut heavily re-entrant curves, or even to cut circles in the glass for insertion, first cut the line you hope to achieve, having left all the other lines of the cutting till later (this gives the glass greater strength and resistance to fortuitous cracks). Then cut many criss-crosses, the more the better, forming a lattice of starts within the area to be cleared of glass. Gently tap the perimeter start, so that it is fairly deep; this will prevent any of the subsidiary starts from overshooting the mark and going beyond where they

should, because they will be stopped by the transverse cut. Then diligently tap away at the centre till it looks somewhat like a shattered windscreen. The centre soon becomes so loose that you can either watch it fall out or gently pull it out with the pliers, a little at a time.

A curve can be effected by a series of ever-deepening segments of curve eating into the glass —each one tapped and removed with the pliers. This is not so satisfactory, because of the pressure that is liable to build up against each end of the remaining glass. This may, in the end, overpower the glass and cause it to crack in the middle of the piece you wish to retain.

If you have a small piece of glass to break off— or a thin strip of glass that it is impossible to break with the fingers—the plate pliers come into their own. When using plate pliers be careful not to pinch the glass too hard, otherwise it will tend to shatter under the pressure. Old glaziers sometimes hold the glass in a fold of their apron, between the surface of the glass and the inner jaws of the plate pliers, to make sure of not pinching the glass. Hold the pliers with your index finger between the two halves of the handle, and break and pull away in one movement.

In cutting a slice of glass or a long strip in two, it is sometimes best to employ two plate pliers together, holding one half of the glass in one, and the other half in the other, at the thick end of the glass—if there *is* a thick end. You will find that the cut in almost all cases runs down the piece of glass in a firm clean break, giving you exactly the shape you need.

Never forget to place your glass on the pattern of the cutline in such a manner as to minimize waste. With extra difficult shapes always start at the most difficult cut so that in the event of the cut going wrong you have not wasted your previous effort.

Do not try to cut the impossible in glass, by cutting out sharp wedge-shaped angles, or it will break across where it is indicated (*50*). Sharp corners can be cut, but they should be done as shown.

Even if you have made shapes in the cutline that are feasible as far as cutting is concerned, it is

56

well to consider the glazing as part extension of the cutting of them. Are the shapes so bizarre as to look odd when leaded? Will the shapes in fact be impossible to lead because in the end they are too delicate, attenuated, or interlocked? Are some of the curves on the lines of the glass so trivial and incidental that they will eventually get flattened out or swallowed up in the cruder outlining of the lead?

Finally, if the glazing *is* a possibility round such shapes, are some of the pieces of glass cut in such a way as to stand up to the natural strains of wind-pressure over the years beating on the window, or the stress of being put into the window, and being handled by men who have not made the window?

All these questions are worth asking yourself before undertaking the sweat of cutting bizarre or unnecessarily complicated shapes.

Special cutting

Certain glasses need careful handling because of their optical qualities, not their physical ones. These are principally as follows:

1 *Glass too dark to see through*, therefore rendering the light-box useless. In the Continental method, this is no problem, since the cut-out template can be used. In the English method there are two ways of dealing with it. The first is the simpler: that is to slip a piece of carbon paper between the cutline and the glass (the cutline and the glass positions are the reverse of normal) with the carbon side of the paper face down to the glass. Trace with a pencil round the cutline perimeter of the glass you want to cut; this transfers a small greasy line of carbon to the glass. Dust the glass over with the pounce bag and the line will show up white. Follow the line with the cutter.

Another way is to leave the dark glass to one side for cutting right at the end of the whole job, and cut thin plain glass templates in 18 or 24 oz glass. When all the rest of the glass is cut, you may pounce round the perimeter of the thin templates held against the dark glass, and then remove the thin white glass template and cut along the division line of dark glass (the shape you want) and pounce (the shape you will discard).

2 *Very thick dark glass* can be cut by scoring two lines, one outer and one inner, and tapping the outer and grozing into the inner line with the plate pliers.

3 *Flashed glass* Although there is usually, apart from questions of annealing, no trouble in cutting flash glass, it is worth while asking yourself whether, in the process of painting (which includes aciding) you want the flash side to be towards the inside of the building or the outside. If the flash is to be acided and painted, the effect will be entirely different, according to which way round it is. Flash glass is usually best cut on the base-side, so that it may be necessary, if the flash is required on the inside, for the cutline to be entirely reversed and the glass cut in reverse, always remembering to re-reverse the cutline after the passage has been cut.

4 *Double-flash cutting* As an extension of the last paragraph, if there is a passage in the stained glass that needs to be double-acided, or acided on one half of the plating, and if you do not want the aciding to go on the outside of the window because it looks unsightly, cut one acided flash (the outer one) in reverse, then re-turn over the cutline and cut the other in the ordinary way, so that when both of the acided flash surfaces are up on the easel they are facing inwards to each other and in register. Similarly it is as well, when cutting slab or any violently irregular glass, to consider on which side of the window the violent irregularity would be best placed, and to reverse the cutline if necessary. If you have cut slabs and irregular glass in reverse, by reversing the cutline it is as well to mark the cutline REVERSE GLAZE: this will prevent the bumps lifting the body of the leaded up panel away from the glazing bench when the time comes. It is easy to begin glazing only to be caught out by something impossible.

5 *White commercial flashed glass and opalescent glass* These glasses have two curious properties, possibly connected with their opalescence. They are resistant to acid, and they are very soft in the fire.

51 *Dark glass cutting using clear glass template and pounce-bag technique*

52 *Dark glass cutting using carbon-paper and pounce-bag technique*

Though it is difficult to acid them, these glasses are affected by acid fumes which pit and pore the surfaces. This means that they are likely to pick up all kinds of extraneous dirt, especially the black off the cementing table. If any kind of sand-blasted glass is used, it must be protected by being reverse cut and having a template cut out of white glass which will ensure that the sandblasting will not sully up in the course of work. Owing to the capillary action of the oil in putty, sometimes this seeps into the gap between the protective template and the sandblasted sheet—destroying effectively for good the granular, opalescent effect of the sandblasting. So *bind* the two glasses together with scotchtape before glazing.

6 *Exceptionally hard glass* All reds and a few yellows seem to be quite extraordinarily hard and difficult to cut; the flashed reds being impossible to cut except on the base-glass, more or less solve their own problems—but the cadmium and selenium reds, which are not flashed, but pot, are extremely difficult. The best way of cutting is to guide the cutter firmly along the line, having laid the cutline down flat on the table, with the glass on it, and at the same time press the end of the

almost perpendicular handle with the thumb or forefinger of the left hand. You will notice the curious indifference of the glass towards being cut —practically no mark and practically no noise, no impression at all in fact. But a small tap will reveal that one cutting operation is enough, and that where it seemed that nothing had happened it is not after all necessary to go over the cut with the cutter a second time. I should add that it is extremely difficult to effect smooth curving cuts in this hard red and yellow glass. The cutter seems to jerk ahead in a straight line just where you do not want it to go.

General discipline of cutting

Unless there is some method in cutting there is bound to be a great deal of mess round the cutting table. A few general rules of conduct will help.

1 Select what glass you want from the racks; if you are in doubt about the colour, and want more colours than will in fact be used, it is usual to put them suitably stacked in the studio window, to have a look at them (having previously marked each piece of glass with the appropriate rack number).

2 Do not accumulate large pieces of glass in piles against the legs of the table, or anywhere where they can be accidentally damaged.

3 The middle-sized pieces of glass, and the smaller pieces, can be put in a small wooden toast-rack-like holder on the cutting table; this is quite easily made, and enables the glass that is wanted to be selected very quickly.

4 When cutting plating, or a second piece of glass that is to be leaded up together with its similar shape, it is better to cut the darkest plating first, and put it on the easel or plate glass. The reason for this is that though you need to see the effect of the colour the first time the glass is mounted in the studio window, the extra physical thickness of the plating is a nuisance when you come to paint. When you are ready to paint, remove the lighter plating on top, paint the lower plating, and then lead up, having reversed the two pieces of glass (so that the painted surface is to the inside of the window, not sandwiched in between the glass).

5 When each piece of glass has been cut it is a good idea to mark the place on the cutline with a small dab of red or blue wax pencil; this prevents the irritating occurrence of doubling up in cutting when you do not intend to.

6 Further to this, the pieces of plating that you cut should be marked with a cross on the top (lightest) piece, as you put it on the plate-glass panel. This makes it easier to distinguish plating from ordinary glass once it is set up in the studio window.

7 The cutline should be marked with a 'P' in red wax chalk so that, in the course of leading, the sight of the cutline will warn you that plating is coming, and you will be able to make provision for it.

8 When cutting tracery lights fix a large-scale paper clip to the edge of the table so that the cutlines of the tracery are secure in it and hang down by your side in a convenient position.

The cutlines may be removed one at a time as you cut from them. After cutting the glass to any one tracery it is best to put the cutline *either* on the tray containing that particular cut glass or in a separate pile as having been done. Otherwise it is very easy to cut a piece of tracery twice over.

Policy of cutting

Do not think that it is possible either to get the right colour straightaway, or, unless it is to be an entirely unpainted window, to make a complete artistic statement in the process of cutting. More than a certain amount of time spent cutting will distract from the amount of insight and energy left over for the art of painting of the art of anything else for that matter. It is far better to do the whole first cut on the supposition that first decisions will be right, and have a look at the whole window in context when it is up, rather than suffer a crisis of artistic conscience over the exact selection of each colour the first time you cut. In the former case, you are making a unified artistic decision over a broad field; in the latter you are exhausting yourself with many decisions which are too small in themselves to be conclusive, and may well be quite beside the point when seen all together.

Therefore it is a good rule not to look too often at your panel when you are cutting it. Cut it quickly, get it up, have a look, then make a conclusive artistic judgment when it is possible to judge all the colours in relationship to one another. Even one piece of glass can lead to a distortion in your judgment of the whole composition.

If this method of cutting becomes a habit, it will build up the faculty of visually imagining in your own mind the effect of colour in the first glass. This is a kind of parallel to the art of composing by writing in a manuscript and the art of composing by sitting at the piano—both are valid, but ultimately the former yields greater results.

Painting, Staining, Aciding and Plating

Why paint on glass? As it has been rather naively stated 'you've got to put in the drawing and the shading', i.e. if a fully three-dimensional effect is needed—which God forbid—it is impossible to do anything about it except by means of painting. But that is to carry things to extremes. It cannot be that the effect of the final window depends on the contrast between highly painted passages and highly clear passages. This obviously is licit, but I would observe that it is usually fatal to end the painted form on the edge cutline (encapsulating the painted image in a lead, in fact). An immediate dichotomy between the painted and unpainted portion is apparent, and before you know where you are you are dealing with two divergent aesthetics, and you are un-aware how to cope with the situation. My advice is to let the painted passage flow over the periferal leads even if only intermittently or for a very short distance. The resultant *image* will then dominate the lead (as it should) instead of being itself dominated. Occasionally a complete matte can be spread over a window and only cleared in places. Again, the paint can be very firmly and thickly applied leaving large areas of clear glass be-tween. Some of the best quality paints for stained glass come from Holland. Very fine dark bistres, umbers and black. I know little of Belgian and German colours for glass-painting but bearing in mind the excellence of Belgian artist's colours and the sophistication of German porcelain painting colours, I think they would be well worth investi-gating.

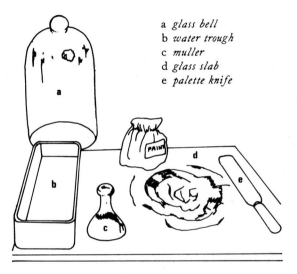

a *glass bell*
b *water trough*
c *muller*
d *glass slab*
e *palette knife*

53 Tools for the painting of glass

When the stained glass has been cut and fixed to the easel or plate glass, and is set up at the end-window of the studio, the first thing to do is to study the colour with reference to the colour cartoon, if there is one.

Go over the glass with an oyster knife, and remove all the pieces of glass that are not in accordance with the colour, rhythm, and tonal scheme of the window, and re-cut them. The re-cutting can either be done after all the unwanted glass is removed, or, as I prefer, by removing a few pieces at a time and replacing them with re-cut pieces. Once the window is up it can be enhanced by:

I Painting IV Plating
II Staining V Enamelling
III Aciding VI Fusing superimposed pieces

Of these six ways of varying the glass, the first two are the most important.

I *Painting*

Paint for glass consists of a mixture of finely levigated glass dust, iron oxide, sometimes various other metal oxides, and a flux, possibly borax, which enables the glass dust to melt on to the glass surface and fuse with it, without the glass itself melting and running away. The paint frits at a lower temperature than the vehicle glass.

There are many formulae for glass paint. It is difficult to say which is the best from the point of view of durability. All the manufacturers claim to have the best, but there are differences in handling, covering power, density, opacity, transparency, and colour. Also a difference in performance in the kiln. Some paints come up in minute bubbles, called pin-holes, some draw together in blobs. The paint behaves similarly to china and pottery paint, though it is fired at a lower temperature.

There are different qualities of paint, some especially smooth-running and dense for tracing lines on glass, others of different colours, ranging from blue-grey to brown, through khaki and black.

While it is always a good idea to experiment with different paints and form one's own judgment, the paints most useful are those that:

(a) mix easily in the gum and water;
(b) flow easily from the brush;
(c) give a pleasant colour when transparent against the light;
(d) give a pleasant finish to the interior surface of the glass when the window is illuminated by electric light at night.

A black paint that goes faintly neutral-tinted-blue when diluted with water and used very thinly, is the best paint for ordinary use. Some blacks are very stable and well behaved, others are apt to pin-hole in the fire very badly.

Paint can be mixed in a variety of ways:

1 The most usual way is with gum and water.
2 Another way is to mix gum and a little acetic acid with the water. This fixes the layer of paint so that it will remain undisturbed by any subsequent wash of paint, enabling the two layers to be fired in one.
3 For final effects on top of the acetic-acid paint and the gum and water paint, an oil-ground paint can be used, diluted with the thinner that is supplied for enamels. This does not affect the water-bound paint underneath, and all three layers can be fired at the same time. Unrefined genuine turpentine that has been left out to partially evaporate is a good medium for this paint.

The acetic acid mixed paint is very good for tracing, as it is undisturbed by what goes on, on top of it. Naturally the oil-bound paint is the last to go on to the glass before it is fired, as water-gum-paint will not settle on an oily surface, and separates out.

The use of different methods of painting in series, one after the other, has everything to commend it in theory, but generally speaking it is not the way an artist works today. The present-day handling of art materials is the simple one of using the plain gum-water paint. It is direct, subtle, and fresh in handling, whereas the more complicated methods of painting can get extremely involved and over-worked. The result of over-working is an appearance of elaboration and dryness.

Equipment

Every artist makes up his own mind about his equipment, or rather his hand makes his mind up for him, but the following list of brushes is given as a rough guide.

1 *Broad hog or other stiff-haired brushes* From 152 mm to 25 mm (6 in. to 1 in.) wide. These come under the heading of tradesmen's brushes. The bristles are from 38 mm to 63 mm ($1\frac{1}{2}$ in. to $2\frac{1}{2}$ in.) long, the brushes can be quite flat from front to back, or wider. I prefer the extra width because of the extra power of holding the

54 Head of a man at Marsh Baldon church, Oxfordshire.
    Fourteenth century

62

55 *Detail from head of St James the Great. Victoria and Albert Museum. Fifteenth century*

56 *Detail from window designed by Marc Chagall, Tudely, Kent, England*

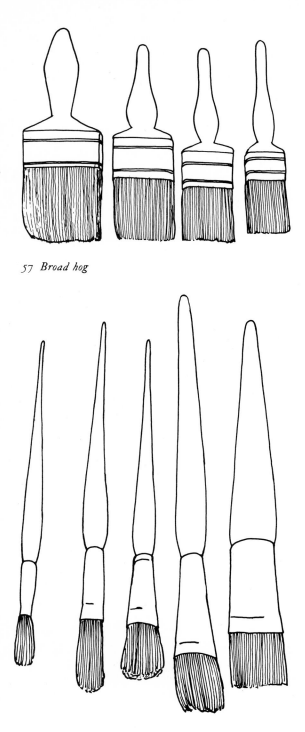

57 *Broad hog*

58 *Oil-colour brushes*

paint, so that the supply of paint does not run out half-way through a stroke. It may be objected that these brushes are too heavy and clumsy for the kind of work that is done on stained glass. I have found just the opposite. After all it is perfectly possible to have a light and delicate touch with heavy brushes, but the opposite, i.e. making an emphatic statement with light-weight brushes, is impossible. The touch in this sort of brush varies from the most delicate sustained wash, through many different kinds of texturing and stippling, to the boldest and blackest of strokes. But a really good quality of brush and bristle must be used. Ordinary house-painting brushes will not do, as they have no flexibility in their bristles.

2 *Oil-colour brushes* A variety of flat, filbert-headed, and long hog-bristled oil-colour brushes are useful for certain work. They have a very good quality of touch. In England the quality of Hamilton and George Whiley brushes of this type are the best, but for stained glass they tend not to hold enough paint to continue a stroke for sufficiently long.

3 *Soft oil colour brushes* The kind of brushes that in France are sold as calves-hair brushes (*de veau*), if they have sufficiently long hair are sensitive and good. They vary in width from 19 mm to 28 mm ($\frac{3}{4}$ in. to $1\frac{1}{8}$ in.), and a set is worth having.

4 *Water-colour brushes* These very expensive (usually sable or sable-mix) brushes generally speaking I find quite useless for painting on glass.

5 *Broad-headed, flat, soft-haired brushes* There are times when the delicacy of touch in these brushes is useful, but they have many disadvantages. The paint tends to drag the tip of the brush into a bunch—the broader the original brush when dry the denser the bunch when wet. The brush then tends to split into groups of hair, so that two or three parallel lines or impressions are made on the glass where only one was intended. These brushes dry up quickly and have to be replenished with paint very often; they tend to drip water at the handle and soon start to lose

59 *Broad, flat, soft brushes*

hairs. Still, with all these drawbacks, it is worth having one or two to hand. They are very useful when dealing with enamels, which are ground in an oil base.

6 *Riggers, liners, pencils* These long, thin, flex-ible-haired brushes are most valuable. Not only for drawing, hatching, shading, and generally crispening, but for the fluent quality of their touch. Much glass painting technique today suffers from a feeling of stodgy claustrophobia in its handling, whereas the use of long-haired brushes releases the hand into some kind of spontaneity of action.

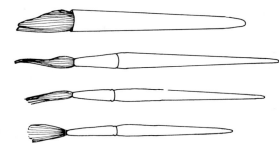

60 *Riggers, liners, and pencils*

7 *Small, long quill brushes* These may generally be too weak to be of any use in glass painting, but there are occasions when they might be worth-

while. It is worth getting two or three and seeing how they suit your hand and your style.

8 *Chinese brushes* Chinese brushes are, nowadays, the nearest thing to the original brushes used in the glass painting of the Middle Ages. The larger and the more robust the brush, the better it is for stained glass. The smaller, more delicate, brushes are apt to get clogged by the weight of paint; this makes them fill out and become stodgy in handling. Middle-sized and large Chinese brushes are, without a doubt, the most versatile. They are extremely flexible and can be used equally in quick brilliant passages of drawing or texture, or sus-tained line work, or in the traditional Chinese way of painting that takes full advantage of their being able to produce wedge-shaped strokes. Chinese brushes hold the paint very well, never letting more than sufficient come out at the end whilst painting, but, at the same time, having a great deal of paint in reserve for sudden emphasis if this is needed. They produce an exceedingly sharp and brilliant quality of brush work. They seem ideally made for that kind of succinct spon-taneity that should be the hallmark of good glass painting. Moreover, they are very long-lasting, justifying the initial expense. Goat hair is prefer-able to hog.

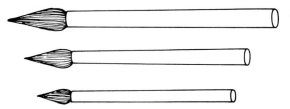

61 *Chinese brushes*

9 *Other brushes* Any other brushes that the painter cares to experiment with can be put into use. Such things as tooth-brushes, cut-down house-painter's brushes, cut-down oil brushes, are useful. It depends on the painter's hand. In the course of many years of work, you will find that your hand gets used to surprisingly few instru-ments, and can draw out the most varied effects by using the minimum of tools.

10 *Badger brushes* One of the most important

65

62 *Badger brushes*

of all tools I have left till last. The badger brush, which is the last survivor of the badger brushes used in all painting and coachwork in the past, is kept on for use in stained glass. In glass-painting you are working with a transparent medium and your positive statements in the medium are more often than not with the positive light let *in* to the window. A matt of paint smoothed over by the badger is ready to be treated in a variety of ways to let the light in through the dull matt. Letting the light in is the essence of glass painting, hence the persistence of the badger.

The badger can be 102 mm (4 in.) wide at the ebony ferrule, but since the badger hairs spread out in a bushy sort of way, the ends of the badger brush are that much wider. The hairs are anything up to 63 mm (2½ in.) long, and the great characteristic of badger hair is that as well as being very flexible it is completely unaffected in elasticity by water and retains its spring for upwards of forty years. It is safe to say that if the badger is properly cared for, it will last two lifetimes.

Since the badger is used to manipulate the paint when it is already on the glass, it is quite unnecessary to get it wet except at the tips. Occasionally it needs a wash, but only once a week or so. The best way of giving it a dry clean is to flip the ends of the hairs rapidly backwards and forwards across a square chairleg.

A large badger, because the hair that goes into it is so rare and has to be hand-selected, is extremely expensive to buy nowadays.

Smaller badgers can be obtained—76 mm, 50 mm, or 25 mm (3 in., 2 in., or 1 in.) wide, or round ones about 12 mm (½ in.) in diameter.

Generally speaking, choose ones with the longest possible hairs, they will last longer, the hairs being of the best quality, and they will repay their prodigious expense many times over.

The badger brush as supplied by **Hamilton's** is very good indeed being rather firmer and less 'whippy' than the equivalent German brush. I prefer the English, but there will be those who prefer the German because it has far finer, softer, more gentle, more voluptuous a touch. It simply depends on the type of work you do or the character of the painting.

Miscellaneous equipment
For working on the glass after painting, a variety of small stiff brushes, pot cleaners, wooden sticks for picking out lines with, metal needles, rollers, goose and turkey quills, feathers, odd pieces of rubber—the list is endless, and depends solely on the ingenuity of the individual artist and what he feels he wants to say.

The large trinity window in the church at Stretford, just outside Manchester, painted by Geoffrey Clarke, is the only instance I know of a stained-glass window being entirely painted by means of rollers rather than brushes.

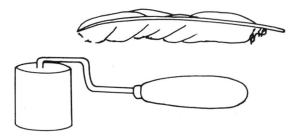

63 *Additional painting tools*

Special effects
The execution of special effects is dealt with on pages 74–8, but it is as well to have a stock of the following:

Broad roll of transparent adhesive tape or masking tape

Tube of rubber-latex glue, e.g. Copydex
Small roll of polythene sheet
Various kinds of paper, from newspaper to tissue
Some corrugated cardboard
Small bottle of thick turpentine (*not* turps substitute).

Mixing the paint

Painting on stained glass depends on one extremely simple thing, and one only. In this it is akin to water-colour and to Chinese calligraphic painting, and to nothing else in the technique of painting. It is all a question of judging how much water to mix with the paint, and assessing the rate at which the paint is drying on the glass as the hand works over it. There is nothing more to the whole technique than that, yet it takes a lifetime to be sensitive to it.

The first thing to do is to mix the paint properly and homogeneously.

The palette

Any sheet of plate glass will do as a palette, though I have found that a good large sheet of 12 mm ($\frac{1}{2}$ in.) ground glass is the most satisfactory. The edges of course have to be well ground and smoothed off. There is something about the weight and substance of this thickness of glass that gives confidence and steadiness to the hand as it stretches out to replenish the brush. When painting, the last thing you want is the sensation of stretching out to something flimsy, wobbly, and expendable. Heavy plate glass is a bore to move; however, once it is moved it does not get leant on, tipped over, shoved to one side, and generally put in the way of danger—leading to its being broken.

A palette of about 46 cm × 38 cm (18 in. × 15 in.) is ideal. This enables the colour to be ground (if necessary) on it and the pile of paint that has been made ready should be covered by a glass bell or a round tin to keep in the right amount of moisture.

Method

Pile the powdered paint into a heap in the middle of the palette. Using a large palette knife or spatula, make a hole in the middle so that it looks like a volcano. Put a little water in the hole and tip the sides down towards the hole, when they will fall into the water and crumble. Now add a quarter to a third of the amount of liquid pure gum arabic to the muddy pool in the middle. Finally, add a little more water and turn the edges into the middle again. Repeat this, not overdoing the water, until you have a homogeneous mixture. To mix the paint more smoothly, a series of vertical parallel cuts through the paint with the palette knife, followed by an underscrape and a plop on top of the pile, will help. Repeat as many times as is needed.

When the paint is well mixed for handling, it will have the quality of being what can only be described as well set up. It will not be runny and liquid, nor will it be solid and stodgy. It will feel rather as though it were slightly in suspension. Paint mixed to this consistency will be easy to handle on the brush; it can be diluted with a watery brush, but may also be used neat if a heavy passage of painting is needed, or if tracing is being done.

Faults

Too much or too little water.
Too little mixing.
Too much or too little gum.

After a little practice, it should be quite easy to get just the right amount of gum in the paint. Too much makes the paint dry brick-hard on the glass, when it cannot be worked at all, either by the badger when half-dry, or with the needle or pick when wholly dry.

Too little gum is not noticeable until the glass is either attempted to be painted over a second time before being fired for the first time, or is fingerprint and scratch when put into the kiln. Either way, the effect looks moth-eaten and must be re-done.

Messy or untidy palette.

This might not seem important, but it is. If the palette is left with mudruts of paint all over it and the ruts are allowed to dry, it will be virtually impossible to mix the paint (say the next day) without getting it fouled with broken-off lumps from the surrounding caked paint. This will produce an unpleasant granular effect, and start bad habits of painting. When the paint is well mixed up, if it is not going to be used immediately the palette should be cleaned thoroughly all round the pile of paint in the middle with a damp cloth; then the bell should be placed over the pile, leaving some paint on the outside; finally, a rather watery brush that has previously been lightly dipped in the paint, should quickly be drawn all round the rim of the glass bell, where it meets the palette, sealing all the moisture inside it. When the paint is needed, a gentle but firm tap on the side of the bell with the open palm of the hand will release it, and the paint will be found to be fresh as when it was first mixed, even after a week.

Water container

A fairly wide-necked bottle (an English half-pint glass milk bottle) is an ideal container for water to be mixed with the paint. A long dish, such as a glass oven dish, is very useful for a normal water trough in which to dip the brushes. I use one about 90 mm wide, 50 mm deep and 254 mm long (3½ in. wide, 2 in. deep, and 10 in. long); and apart from the sloshing of the water from end to end when it is carried, have found it excellent. Certain brushes are best soaked beforehand to make them more supple. A row of them can be put in this water-trough. Make certain they are well shaken before use, as water can suddenly descend from a secret cachement in the ferrule when you are painting, with distressing results. A stable bowl for water about 15 cm (6 in.) in diameter is a worthwhile addition to the painting table.

Different palettes

Quite obviously it is not necessary to work with one paint only. You can experiment with a number of different mixtures, but my advice is to find out which one you particularly like, and to stick to it. Much messing about with the cookery of painting only emphasises one aspect of stained glass that is complicated enough already.

Methods

As I have said on page 66 the great thing to remember in painting is that the positive statement is *not* predominantly made by the paint, but by the degree and quality and placing of the light left over. If you take a piece of brown paper and pin-hole it, and hold it up to the light, you will notice the pattern of the pin-holes, not the quality of the brown paper. It is exactly the same in painting stained glass. Art students and painters, being used to making positive statements in paint, find this hard to grasp at first. The paint is largely a negative thing.

Given a piece of glass there are really only two methods of painting:

One is by putting a matt or series of matts over the glass and working back towards the light; this is the fifteenth- and sixteenth-century method of working, and is still valid today—recently (i.e. twenty years ago) many of the nave windows of Coventry Cathedral nave were painted in this way by Geoffrey Clarke, Keith New, and Lawrence Lee.

The other is by starting with the clear glass, and only putting on as much paint as is needed to qualify and subdue, and to guide the essentially glittering surface of the glass.

The first method is less spontaneous, but produces an effect of great integration and firmness of design, and it is interesting to note that it is used more by those artists who are attracted by extremely clear and firm linear design. Great delicacy in the use of successive tonal washes can produce an extremely sombre and rich effect.

The second method, which I favour, is more spontaneous, leaves more to chance and accident, and gives a heightened play and glitter to the surface of the glass. Moreover, it does not look dull or faded in back-light or artificial light when viewed from the interior at night, say.

At a distance, the matt-system window holds its light on the window plane and holds it in reserve; whereas the free-painted window is more inclined to halate and shower its light on to the surrounding masonry and the floor.

These two methods of painting glass are of course attacking the same problem from different ends, but this is not to say that they eventually meet in the middle. The two effects remain entirely different, even when carried to their logical extreme, i.e. a heavily painted window is entirely different in effect and in feeling from a heavily matted window. And a lightly painted window is entirely different in feeling from a matted window which has been largely scraped out with scrapers and needles to let in the light. The two methods could conceivably be used in junction, i.e. for different parts of the same window. That is entirely up to the artist; but I think it is virtually impossible to combine the two methods, i.e. paint one way first and then superimpose another: the result would be an awful mess.

Two positions of painting
Upright This is the traditional method of painting after the main line-tracing had been done and allowed to dry. More control of water and brushwork is needed because there is a tendency for the paint to slide, or weep, down the glass. Practice will enable the painter to prevent this happening, but the following ways can help.

1 By working on glass that is warmed up either by the sun or artificially with an electric blower or, say, a hand hair dryer. This is tricky, as the individual films and touches of paint dry immediately, which means that any physical, and, usually, artistic amalgamation between the various stages of the painting of the glass is extremely difficult to bring off. The paint remains in a series of hard-edged, independent, overlapping areas. An attempt to put things right by means of scraping out and washing out usually ends in disaster.
2 The use of a small hand hair-drier can be an advantage, because it allows the paint to flow freely and to be fixed, when ready, by means of a blast of hot air from the drier. This can be done successfully with two applications of paint, but succeeding applications are apt to harden round the edges.

Switch of panel of glass from vertical to horizontal
This is obviously impractical if you are using a wooden sliding easel on the mullions. Time cannot be spent switching easels around, even with help, but with the system of individual panels of stained glass on rubber-washered screws the painting can be done largely in the vertical and rapidly be moved from its position if it looks as if the paint is going to run. It may even be an advantage, in some techniques, to let the paint run so far, and then check its progress by turning into the horizontal. When it is horizontally placed it can be left to dry on its own or with the help of a hair-drier.

It is a good idea to work on the whole window at the same time if possible: this means that one part of the window might well be drying horizontally, while the other part is being painted vertically. When the horizontally rested panels are dry, they can be put up again, and worked on in the vertical without loss of time.

Horizontal
The advantages of painting horizontally are the very smooth and even quality of the matt and the sure way of controlling its tonal quality; the evenness of traced lines, and the control of their thickness and thinness; the muffled and velvety quality of any painting put on top of the matt before it has dried. The latter because the edges of the painted portion coming into contact with the water of the matt on the glass, fuzz and blurr a little through dissolution. It also allows for special accents, such as blobs, features, stippling, and textures, to remain where they are placed, and neither to move about nor to change their character.

General observations
Stained glass painting is more flexible than has been described above. Obviously, both methods —matt and painted—have advantages, and can be combined in part, though usually they are not in practice, owing to the temperament of the individual painter. Similarly, so far as the position of the glass is concerned, it is a good idea not to be attached to any one method. The switching of the

glass from vertical to horizontal in the course of painting becomes, in time, automatic if necessity dictates it. The painter develops an instinct as to how far to go.

Techniques

Individual methods are shown in the series of close-ups of paintwork later in this chapter. However, there are one or two techniques of handling that are better described first.

Tracing

In the days of artists who prepared the cartoons, and journeymen-painters who executed the painting to the cartoons' design, tracing was a far more common practice than it is now. I hardly ever trace because I believe there is more life in the free-drawn brush-stroke, even though it is not as accurate as one perhaps would like it to be, than in the most carefully copied line following the exact line of a cartoon. This is a matter of temperament of course, and not necessarily to be followed by everyone. Accordingly here is a good method of tracing if you want to do it.

(a) Put the stained glass horizontal, exactly over the cartoon.

(b) Make sure that all the pieces of glass on the passage to be traced are evenly set on the plasticine, and that edges do not tip up or stand proud. It may be necessary to grind one or two sharp edges so that they do not damage the brushes or impede the smoothness of their progress.

(c) Make sure that the glass is quite free from either grease or water. If there is a spot of grease on the glass, naturally the traced line will not take on it. This is more likely to occur if you have been using wax either for fixing the glass to the plate glass or as a stop-out for aciding, and have left the trace of a wax-spot on the stained glass. It can also occur in places where plasticine has been. Because it is a tracing, the line has to be well defined and accurate; the use of the badger to slur over the passage and force the

line into the grease, thus overcoming the drawing-back effect of the grease on the water-base paint (which can occasionally be done in painting) is impossible. No amount of reiteration with the brush stroke will bridge the gap, and the tracing will end up looking heavy and inaccurate with a blemish in the middle. The only remedy is to wash the whole thing, remove the grease with pure alcohol or acetone, and then re-trace.

Occasionally, in the course of work, water blobs get on the stained glass as it is horizontal. These of course should be dried off before tracing, because, if left, they tend to pull the paint of the tracing brush right into themselves, spoiling the outline of the tracing.
Mix the paint as usual, but with rather more gum and a little less water.*

There are special paints made for tracing which are ground extra fine and flow very easily, but all the tracing paints I have seen have usually fired very red and foxy, to the back-light. The effect at night in a lit-up church in the inside is extremely unpleasant. A network of venetian-red lines is seen running all over the dark glossy surface of the glass.

Brushes to use

The longer, finer, and rounder the brushes you use the better. Professional journeymen-painters used to keep their tracing brushes specially carefully in boxes. Obviously the more damage a brush receives, the less likely it is to do the job of tracing. The tracing handles should be long and light.

Quill-mounted brushes, with such names as crow and lark, can often be too flimsy for tracing, and the smaller, thinner ones should be left alone.

* The trade used to put glycerine or sugar in too, to ease the flow.

Methods of handling

The methods of handling in tracing vary very much. The obvious way of painting a line is not difficult, i.e. simply draw the brush tip where you want it. But there are two snags (1) sooner or later the stroke has to come to an end, and it ends when the capacity of the wrist to flex, or the arm to move smoothly, has been fully taken up; (2) the brush, beginning fully charged and with most of the paint in the tip, and being nearly vertical anyway, tends to discharge a great deal of paint to begin with, and less as the stroke goes on, so that what was intended to be a smooth line is a string of irregular bumps.

This can be counteracted by drawing the brush sideways along the path of the tracing, and by leaning the brush over at an acute angle to the stained glass pane. The only drawback is that the underside of the brush (towards the axis of the arm) may well drag a little, causing a small serrated edge on one side while the other side is smooth.

The solution to these troubles is to hold the brush in the hand with the handle pointed away from you, the tip of the brush pointed in towards the chest, and the hand almost folded in upon itself. Tracing by means of a series of sweeping strokes away from the body, holding the brush at an acute angle to the glass (again, naturally, away from the body) will build up, almost by means of a process of lamination, a smooth homogeneous line in which the re-charging of the brush is unnoticeable, and the resulting line fires without any blemishes. A good deal of practice is necessary for this method, but it is well worth acquiring the skill.

It is not necessary to keep to one kind of brush. Large ones or small ones find their appropriate place, but they all should have long 38 mm ($1\frac{1}{2}$ in.) hair or fine bristle.

Matting

The function of the matt is to mitigate the light coming into the window at the window plane. Of all the activities in painting glass, matting is the most important and versatile.

Uses of matting Not only is matting used to phrase the emphasis in the glass, i.e. some passages in stained glass need to be secondary to others; but the whole character of a colour can be given a different relationship with its neighbours by suppressing it with matt or by suppressing the radiance of the surrounding colours. It is the basis for a great deal of paintwork in connection with stippling and picking out with the wooden stick or the metal needle.

A matt can also be employed across a passage of widely different tones and colours—running through the passage *in counterpoint* to the various statements of colour.

Paint for matt This is the same as for painting in general, and should be mixed with perhaps a little more water.

Brushes for matt The best brushes for putting on the paint in broad, even layers, prior to matting, is undoubtedly the broad house-painter's brush, provided it is of really good quality. Soft-haired broad brushes tend to become sloppy and bunchy, and consequently do not spread the paint evenly enough to enable the badger to go over the layer and make it homogeneous.

At the same time, the obvious rule applies: i.e. when the field for matt is large and the individual pieces of glass are large, then the brushes can be broader; and conversely, if the field to be matted is small, then the brushes and the badger should be smaller. In the latter case, soft brushes could conceivably be a help.

The badger is inseparable from the act of matting.

Use a very thin mixture of paint that will remain liquid on the surface of the glass for rather longer than ordinary paint does. It is usually necessary to go over the surface to be matted once or twice in different directions with the paint brush before using the badger. The badger imparts a certain quality which can only be fixed to paint that is already smooth and consistent.

The difficulty in badgering a matt is knowing when to stop. If too much badgering is done on the matt, the paint may dry sufficiently for the badger to act as a picking-off agent, and little light striations will occur. This can be taken advantage of when it is intended, but otherwise it is a nuisance. Usually, because the paint does not dry evenly all at once, you get a hint of what is going to happen, and can then leave the rest of the matting well alone.

Alternatively, you may stop 'whipping' with the badger too soon, in which case, if the glass is vertical, the matt begins to form into tears and furrows down the glass; if the glass is laid horizontal, the character of the matt is lost by the granules of paint aimlessly floating about in the water, victims of any little depression or hillock in the antique glass. In either case the homogeneity is impaired.

Further use of the badger
As well as whipping across the surface, the badger can be used head on to stipple away little pinpricks from the surface of the matt, creating rather the effect of a mezzotint, but in reverse. By skilful use of the badger on the matt, a whole range of subtle shades and tones can be brought into being. The stippling of the matt, by arresting each little area of matt and isolating it on its own has the effect, not only of letting the light in and stopping the glass from looking dead, but of arresting any tendency the matt might have to creep or bunch or distort.

Whipping
The badger can whip mainly in four different ways:
1 With plenty of water in the paint the badger can push the layer of paint around, making light areas in the middle of dark, dark in light, and shading dark into light. To start an initial clear area, the badger may have to be pressed fairly hard, and the side of the bristles used, to push the paint—rather like sweeping with a broom.
2 The paint is mixed with just sufficient water—this produces the ordinary matt.
3 With less water, usually following on the previous state of the paint, the badger becomes partly an instrument to even out the matt, and partly a very delicate picker. A slashing movement of the badger on a matt which is nearly dry can create a beautiful sash of light.
4 The act which is known in the trade as 'whipping' (as opposed to badgering) is a continuous movement of the badger over the field of the matt—a whipping action in which the badger, held lightly over the matt between the base of the thumb and forefinger, is violently oscillated or fanned over the matt. The ends of the badger scarcely touch the paint surface, and there is a definite fanning or winnowing feeling. The result is that the matt gathers into a minute random pattern of clear glass and dense black, which gives a marvellous quality to the light coming through.
5 When the matt is completely dry, it can be overpainted and picked out.

Matting without the use of the badger
By skilful use of a broad sensitive housepainting brush, the whole area of the window can be lightly and delicately matted without a badger at all. Again, this is really a case of judging accurately the water-content of the paint, and leaving off the sweeping brush-strokes when the paint is just gelling, or settling, on the glass. The quality and direction of the brush-strokes must be taken into account—they will scarcely be eliminated. A whole window so matted, if the colour is selected extremely carefully, can look very beautiful.

Painting
All the tools and odd-effect props are capable of being used. By constant use of the paint-brush, you will gradually find out the difference between putting dirt on to the glass—which it always feels like in the beginning—and the painting of the glass.

Here again, it is a question of the exact amount of water that is used in the paint, and the instinctive knowledge of how dry the paint layer is on the glass, or should be, according to what you want to do with it.
1 *Masking, and lift-ground technique* If there is a passage in the window that needs completely clear treatment, next door to one of very violent paintwork, cover the pieces of glass you want to retain unpainted with adhesive tape or masking tape, and with a razor blade or a Stanley knife cut round the shape that you wish to preserve. Paint the appropriate passage, and remove the tape. This method can also be used for defining the

Nuit de Noel by Henri Matisse
Museum of Modern Art, New York
Copyright SPADEM, Paris, 1977

Detail from exhibition panel by
Patrick Reyntiens

area you want to be painted—or for defining an area of heavily matted glass that is required to have hard edges.

On a matt which has dried, any area that is required as a lighter accent on the matt can be marked in water, and matted quickly and lightly over again; the previously watered area will occur in a lighter tone.

Rubber latex glue which has been used as a defining agent for a lift ground area should be used rather thickly, painted *on*, and *between*, and then removed with a pin or a needle. If the latex is not put on very thickly, by the time it becomes rubber the film is so thin that it is difficult to locate under the paint, much less drag it off. If it is left on during the firing, the paint draws together in blobs and lumps. This is difficult to remedy afterwards.

2 *Oil and water techniques* The fact that oil and water will not mix can be utilised for all kinds of treatments and contrasts.

It is far better, if a blobby texture is required, to spread partially evaporated turpentine on the glass with a small sponge or cloth. Then judge the amount of paint and water and very carefully draw the brush swiftly and lightly over the oiled surface. The water-colour paint separates out into droplets. The more generously the paint is loaded on the brush, the larger the blobs will become.

In the course of replenishing the brush, some of the turpentine will drip back onto the palette and start spotting and separating out the paint. This should be avoided, and the only way to do so is to mix up some paint on another palette specially for the job.

A mixture of oil and water can be used on glass to give a mottled effect. But once laid on the glass (usually horizontally), the paint layer must not be disturbed by the badger, otherwise the effect will become nondescript and blurred.

3 *Oil-ground paint* on top of a wet layer of water-colour-ground paint does not work. Trying to float oil-ground paint on a bath of water for the effects of marbling does not seem to work either, as the paint, being heavy, sinks to the bottom.

Firing out
Some of the substance of the paint disappears in the course of firing. When the trays are first taken out, the paint can have changed considerably; this is described in the next chapter, but it is worth while saying here that the act of re-painting restores what has already been first painted and been partially lost in the firing, and the second firing does not injure the crispness of the paint in the same way as the first.

64 *All Souls window, Derby Cathedral. One of two windows designed by Ceri Richards and made by Patrick Reyntiens, showing the effects possible in painting and aciding*

65 *Chinese brush*

67 *Splattering with Chinese brush*

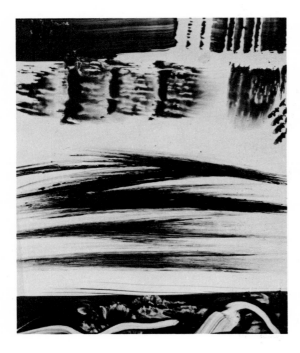

66 *Brush strokes with Chinese brush*

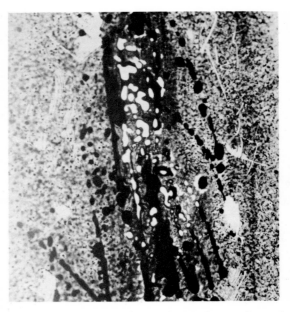

68 *Chinese brush splatter over badgered matt. Some of the brush strokes are rubbed away in the centre whilst still slightly damp leaving counter-change effect*

74

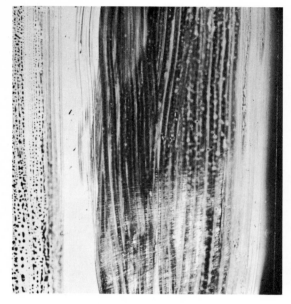

69 *Water-oil mixture showing mottled effect in matt. Badger-brushed at the bottom of the photograph*

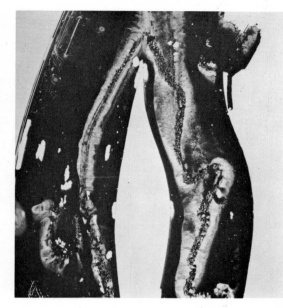

71 *Effect of broad brush strokes over lines of soldering tallow*

70 *Copydex pattern on glass*

72 *Same pattern, dried, matted, and badgered, then Copydex pulled off revealing counter-change*

73 *Matt, very watery, laid (horizontally) over a layer of thick turps already on the glass*

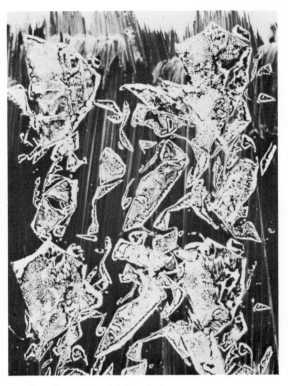

75 *Decalcomania with bunched-up newspaper*

74 *Decalcomania with newspaper using deliberate crease in paper*

76 *Decalcomania with cloth bunched up, showing more velvety effect than with paper*

77 *Decalcomania with bunched-up polythene*

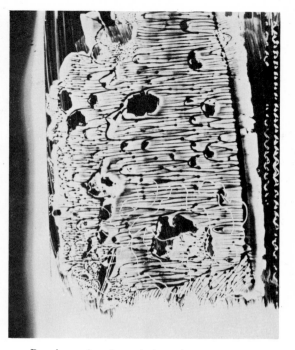

79 *Decalcomania using polythene sheet over a matt*

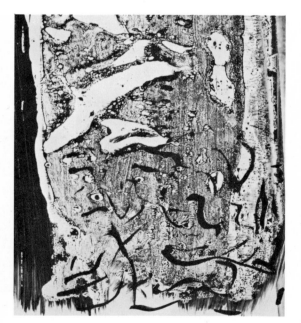

78 *Decalcomania with tracing paper*
   Chinese brush strokes superimposed at the
   bottom of the photograph

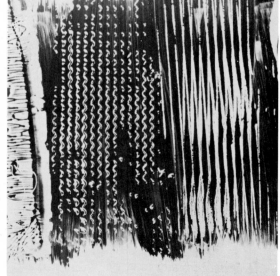

80 *Two blottings on badgered matt*
   a *with corrugated cardboard*
   b *with pressed packing paper*

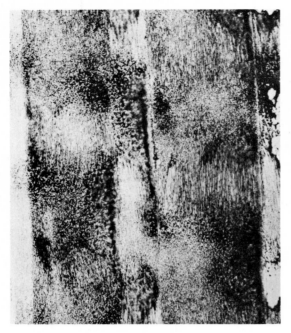

81 *Effect of using rubber sponge roller*

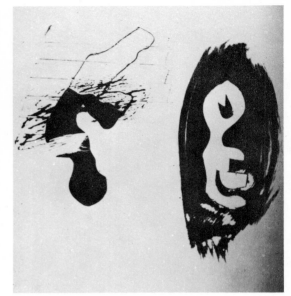

83 *Two figures, using transparent adhesive tape as a stopping-out agent for silhouettes. Tape is removed before firing or re-painting*

82 *Transparent adhesive tape mask with oil-water technique on top. Mask removed leaving clear glass which can then be painted*

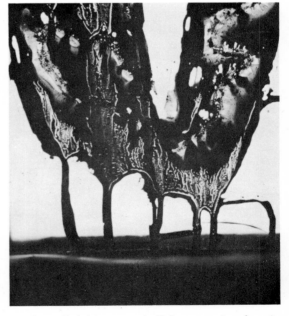

84 *Controlled drip—note the light penetrating the paint*

II Staining

The 'stain' from which the generic name of 'stained glass' is derived was discovered in the early fourteenth century. It was cheap to do and spectacular in results and hence this one process gave its name to the whole art—leading to considerable confusion because laymen think the stained glass artist can stain his glass all the colours of the rainbow. In fact the staining of the basic colours (already cut) in general is only equivalent to putting a variable yellow wash over a particular passage of a painting.

The *stain* that gives stained glass its generic name is a mixture of silver and gamboge with a little gum added.

The action of the silver on the glass is a molecular one. The silver nitrate penetrates the molecules and changes the ionisation of the glass, causing it to filtrate yellow light instead of the white or coloured light it previously did. This explains why stain from the Middle Ages has survived in pieces of stained glass long after the paint has worn off.

All glass is more or less susceptible to stain, but the harder the glass, the less likely it is to stain. In England, some glass is made especially for staining, and nearly all French glass seems to be very sensitive to stain. German glasses are mixed: some of them being good, and some of them indifferent. German white and opalescent glasses are not usually any good for staining at all. In any case this might well be to attempt to gild the lily.

Samples

Because the staining of glass depends on the disposition of the individual coloured glass to take stain, it is essential to keep a neatly docketed drawer full of samples of colours that have been found sensitive. The samples should be 76 mm (3 in.) long, and should be coated with stain on one end; the stain should graduate from dark to light. This is not difficult if the badger is used to graduate from one side to the other. As stain is extremely varied in its performance, and as the time and the heat in the kiln is extremely important, a diamond-scratched note on the glass-sample, giving the time

and temperature of firing, will be useful for future reference. Owing to the fact that it is extremely difficult to remember which stain sample is for which—I usually do a stain sample preliminary test for each job involving staining I have. The samples can however be kept as a kind of demonstration of possibility: something to stimulate the imagination.

Different stains

There are many different stains on the market, varying from strong to silver (i.e. very light yellow). The strong ones are the only ones worth experimenting with. It is possible to obtain cheap sample packets of stains in order to try them out; and sufficient information can be gained in an afternoon to be of use for years.

Grinding stain

Stain may arrive in a granular form, in which case it has to be ground far more than ordinary paint. Moreover, stain is corrosive, especially when it becomes damp, which means that it should be kept in a ceramic or glass jar, preferably with a glass top. The bottom is apt to drop out of the metal tins the stain is delivered in if they are left open. Nowadays in any case stain is delivered in polythene bags.

Mix exactly the right amount of stain for the job, as it tends to dry very quickly. While it is possible to re-activate old stain it takes a long time

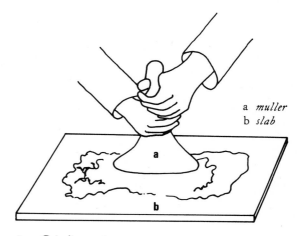

a *muller*
b *slab*

85   Grinding stain

getting it into proper condition and this is almost not worth while.

A small portion of stain is piled on to the middle of the stain palette (a different one, separate from the paint palette), and a hole made in the centre, as for the paint. A very little water is added, the stain falling in towards the centre. When sufficient water has been added, and the stain is set up, it will be noticed that it is in a very granular condition. Now comes the tedious task of grinding the stain further with a muller on the slab, a small portion at a time. The spatula or palette knife is useful to move the stain from place to place. Grinding should be carried out in the way shown in the diagram.

Getting the grain under the muller is not easy and may seem a fruitless occupation, but the finer the stain is ground the better the final results are —and the more controllable and predictable.

An additional method of grinding is that of reducing the stain to powder in a mortar and pestle before mixing it with water. After this has been done the final reduction of the stain under the muller is very much easier.

Once the stain is ground fine enough, it will appear on the palette very much as the paint appears, i.e. 'set up': but it will not handle nearly as well from the brush. Luckily this does not really matter, because stain does not call for definitive precision in the same way as paintwork does; it only needs a knowledge of the ultimate strength and colour and tone, which you will be able to gauge from the data in the stain-sample tray.

Tools
A spatula, a badger, and a small selection of brushes are all that is needed. The brushes should be harder-bristled than the paint-brushes. Soft hairs for applying stain are generally useless: the stain clogs and clings.

If possible, keep a special badger for staining, which need not be as large as the badger used for painting. Select brushes, where possible, with plastic ferrules, as, owing to the corrosiveness of the stain, metal ferrules rust and wear out very quickly.

Always wash without delay anything metal that has come into contact with stain, otherwise it becomes pockmarked and brittle. In spite of being caustic, stain does not harm the skin very much. It is quite safe.

Technique
Owing to the fact that stain acts through the molecular structure of the glass, and does not constitute a layer of anything added to the glass, it is usual to stain the underside of the glass, i.e., the opposite side to the one that is painted. This operation is not possible at the same time as the painting of the glass because the two applications need firing at different temperatures. The two or three firings of paint should be done before the firing of stain.

The glass may be picked out from the painting panel or easel individually, turned over, carefully wiped free of plaster from the kiln, and painted with the stain in whatever pattern is needed. Stain can be whipped, badgered, and generally worked in a lift-ground, oil and water, masking, and stencilling way, exactly as paint is. It is not so capable of subtlety because it is coarser and less predictable in the fire. It is unnecessary to mix gum, or anything else, with stain, since the gamboge (which starts as bright yellow and is fired away completely) is itself a gum.

In passages of stained glass which depend a great deal on the use of stain, it is useful to have a reversed black lead-line, dotted with plasticine, ready to receive the glass as it comes out of the

86 *Pestle and mortar*

80

last paint-firing of the kiln. An accurate register can then be kept, ensuring the right relationship between the various pieces of glass and ensuring that the pattern you wish to make in stain is not jerky or irregular. All the centre lights of the Coventry Baptistry window had to be reversed in this way. The lights were placed on trestles, in order, and then stained in a very broad manner from top to bottom. They were all fired in one fire and not touched again.

Immediately prior to staining it is helpful to slightly dampen the surface of the glass. As the stain tends to dry off too quickly for comfort, the edges of the stained portion are apt to be unworkable with the brush or the badger in a very short time. This leaves a harsh line between stained and unstained parts of the glass, which may not be what is needed. At the same time too much water is not a good idea, since the glass is more often than not slightly cupped, when reversed from the firing, and this means that the water pools in the middle of the cup causing the stain to register too much in the middle of the individual pieces of glass and not enough round their perimeter.

There is plenty of scope to get more than one colour out of the process of staining in one fire, in the way of diluting the stain, over-staining once this is dry, scratching out, dotting, blobbing, and badgering. If the stain is required to be very strong and very weak on the same piece of glass, the best thing to do is to stain the strong portion with strong stain in one fire, and add the field of weak stain, much diluted; to stain in a second fire. Remember that stain always *develops*, never gets lighter in the course of firing, and is very easily over-fired—this is described in the next chapter.

Staining on flashed glass

Staining is generally possible on flashed glass— surprisingly enough, on both sides. The white in some cases stains better than the flash—in others the flash is more susceptible than the white; exactly the same rules hold as in staining pot antique.
Flashed red, if it is strong, is not affected on the flash side at all: the white side is usually extremely good for staining.

Flashed red, when it is light or salmon-coloured, can be stained on the red side, when the stain seems to over-trump the red ions and induces the red and salmon to turn directly to yellow and bronze colour. In no other colour does this occur.
Flashed blue stains well either side, generally speaking, the French flashed blues, especially, staining an extremely rich, ripe-corn colour where the blue has been removed by acid, and retaining full transparency in the process.
Flashed greens, like greens in general, are surprisingly insensitive to stain on the flash side. They are more susceptible on the white side, but are not very good even then and usually have to be given a second firing.

When the flashed glass has been acided, it is found (particularly in greens) that the edge of the acid-bite is far more sensitive to stain than the flash or the white, halo-ing the green areas in a pretty halo of yellow.

Other flashed glasses behave as expected. Pot-metal glasses also behave as expected, with white going to yellow or burnt sienna, yellow deepening to orange or burnt sienna, orange to brown, blue to green, grey to khaki, mauve to brown-mauve.

In very rare cases it may be necessary to fire the stain on to the glass from on top. Owing to the fact that the gamboge leaves a little scabby deposit, this will combine at times with the half-fluxed paint on the top of the glass and destroy the quality of the paint. The scum left by the stain after firing, if it is on the underside of the glass, is quite easily removed with a watery rag, though sometimes a good hard scrub is needed, under running water. Some stains, particularly the stronger ones such as amber, orange, etc., seem to be mixed with gilder's red bole, instead of gambage, as an excipient: this is very much harder to remove after firing the stain. Considerable effort and force is necessary more often than not.

Stain metalling

Sometimes, as a result of firing very strong stain, there is a hard yellow metallic deposit left on the glass after washing. This is called 'metalling'

87 Stained glass window, one of six at Assy, Haute-Savoie, executed by Paul Bony 1948 to the designs of Georges Rouault. Bony had to use the full extent of stained glass technique to reproduce a facsimile of a painting. Rouault's painting itself was inspired by stained glass

and can be removed by lightly mopping with an acid mop.

III *Aciding*

Though the next two sections have nothing to do with working directly on the glass in paint or stain, they have at times a vital contribution to make to the look of the window—they help to mould it's artistic form. Consequently they are included in this chapter.

Acid is used on stained glass in connection with passages of flashed glass whose thin coloured flash

is required to be removed, leaving two colours showing on the one piece of glass. Flashed glass, so acided, can be used in the stained glass window either by itself, painted and/or stained, or in conjunction with plating of another colour, i.e. pot colour, or in conjunction with another piece of flashed glass, which itself has been acided. Together with plating, aciding extends the scope of the medium far beyond what could otherwise be done. In interpreting coloured cartoons, particularly if the style is painterly with subtle edge values between colours and shifts of tone, aciding is practically indispensable. See the illustration of Georges Rouault's window at Assy (left).

Equipment

The aciding compound consists of an enclosure outside, furnished with a small table on which are the aciding trays, and a large (the larger the better) polythene bath full of water, on the ground. There should be a rack for the acid to keep it out of harm's way, if it is stored in the aciding compartment. There should be facilities for clean water—an outside tap is ideal—and a means of getting rid of the old acid in the baths or trays; a direct soakaway into the ground is best. Let it be a big soakaway. Believe it or not many students, after they have finished work with the acid bath, think nothing of tipping fully charged baths down the lavatory, the sink, even the bath tub, to get rid of them. Nothing could be more naïve. The acid, weak though it may be, first removes the glaze from the sink, bowl or tub, and finally eats into the metal piping.

From time to time you will want to change the water in the bath. This is eventually charged with weak acid, so it should be emptied into the soakaway.

Photographer's plastic developing trays are very good for aciding in—except that sometimes the ribbing on the bottom tends to mark the acided glass with bars of left-over colour (the upstanding plastic ribs tend to inhibit the action of the acid). Plastic developing trays are flimsy and should not be handled with acid in them, for fear of their twitching and upsetting. Plastic trays tend to become brittle after about six months' use, and

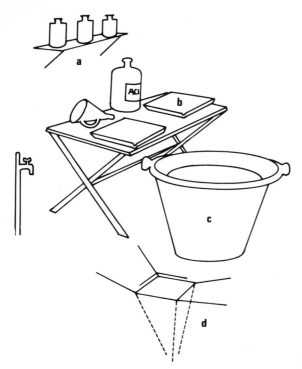

1 A device in which to melt beeswax.
2 A suitable brush.
3 Suitable facilities for cleaning and drying the glass after aciding.

1 The best thing to use for melting the beeswax is a special bath, thermostatically controlled, in which the temperature of the beeswax never rises beyond the point necessary, and so minimises the risk of fire. Pots of beeswax set to melt on a gas ring or electric ring are extremely dangerous, owing to the propensity—when it gets above a certain temperature—of the beeswax to spontaneous combustion. When this does happen, it is sudden, dramatic, and very difficult to put out, owing to the property of self-generation of oxygen that beeswax possesses. If beeswax ever does catch fire, the immediate thing to do is to cover the pot with a lid of some sort and take the whole thing outside as quickly as possible; you can then immerse the *base* of the pot in cold water, which

88 *Tools for the aciding compound*
  a *shelf*   c *large plastic bath*
  b *developing trays*   d *soakaway*

they are liable to spring leaks; this should be carefully watched.

Other materials that can be used for an acid-bath are lead (but this is liable to corrosion), and any inert material with a heavy and homogeneous coating of bitumen on the inside. These are, at best however, inconvenient substitutes for the plastic trays.

If they are used indoors the trays of acid can be placed in an ordinary chemical fume-chamber, but the plate glass round the sides must be replaced with clear perspex, otherwise they will fog and fur up irredeemably on the inside with the acid fumes. Think twice before you undertake aciding wearing glass spectacles. They might mist up for good on account of the acid fumes. Plastic spectacles are all right.

Stopping out

The equipment needed for stopping out:

89 *Magritte. Panel by Paul Marioni, showing the possibilities of aciding and sandblasting*

rapidly brings the temperature below spontaneous-combustion point, but this is highly dangerous, as if any water gets into the beeswax it explodes into steam and sends incandescent beeswax all over the place. It is best to let it burn out.

2 A series of suitable brushes, which must be preheated in the beeswax before they can be used on the glass; otherwise a cold brush put into hot wax reduces the heat of the wax to an extent that it ceases to be viable as a stopping out agent on the glass. These are kept specially for the job, and not used on anything else.

3 These are largely self-explanatory, but it should be noted that if you immerse the waxed glass overnight in a tub of cold water, the wax layer, which previously may have been difficult to remove by scraping, will be seen to have detached itself and slid off the surface of the glass in the course of the night.

Materials

Hydrofluoric acid is obtained from any wholesale chemistry supply firm. The acid can be bought in the chemically pure state, or the commercial; commercial, being cheaper, is quite good enough, but it is weaker.

Hydrofluoric acid is packed in sealed polythene flasks of the usual intervals of liquid measure, up to 1000 cc or more. In the initial handling of the acid, rubber gloves are a great help, but only in the initial handling. After that, during the process of aciding, the gloves can become a snare and a delusion. If a large amount of acid has been bought, decant it into smaller polythene flasks, which are easier and safer to handle. Use a polythene funnel. Always screw on the top of the large flask again firmly, and when screwed on, wash down the outside with clean water. A plastic visor, such as are used in sawmills, can be an added protection against splashes of acid on the face —though these should not occur.

Stopping-out agents As the etching of glass is the same process as ordinary etching, only somewhat cruder, a stopping-out agent is essential.

Beeswax Pure beeswax is difficult to handle except at high temperatures, and is too brittle to stick to the glass for very long under water.

A mixture of one-third beeswax, one-third sheep tallow (used as flux in glazing), and one-third paraffin-wax is the ideal stopping-out agent. This does not have to be heated as high as beeswax, is easy to manipulate with a brush, and can express anything from the finest line, through all kinds of textures and stippling to a complete mask. It is very painterly under the hand.

The disadvantages of beeswax; it floats off the glass in cold weather *and* if it has not been put on sufficiently hot. But by way of compensation it is extremely easy to get off, once the aciding has been done, by soaking overnight in cold water or by gently scraping it off under a running tap.

Bitumen Bitumen paint, or stove polish with an alcohol solvent base, are efficient stopping-out agents. They adhere very well and are dense and impervious to acid.

The disadvantages of bitumen: it is messy and difficult to get off the glass afterwards. Much work has to be done with turpentine rags. It is filthy to have around the studio, and impossible to get off clothes. It is not nearly as compliant under the hand as the mixture of wax and tallow. *But* if the glass is thick (some flash can be 2 mm ($\frac{1}{16}$ in.) thick) and the piece has to be in the acid-bath for a long time—twenty-four hours or more—then I would opt for bitumen paint every time.

Alcohol-based black is very much better to handle than bitumen paint but has a habit of becoming very brittle in time and flaking off either in the bath or, if left an hour or two, before it even reaches the bath.

I have found Rhind's quick drying stopping-out varnish, as supplied by Cornelissen of 22 Great Queen Street, London WC2, is a very good acid resist. It is made for etching techniques, and suggests that any stopping out varnish for etching could be experimented with by stained glass artists.

Masking There are various ways of masking with lead foil or polythene, using the bitumen or wax as an adherent and cutting the mask with a cutter or a Stanley knife blade afterwards to reveal the glass, before putting it in the bath. Since my style is painterly, I have never concerned myself with this method, but lead foil is highly regarded in the white-acid and embossing trade as a resist and it might well reward experiment.

Latex Rubber-based glues, such as Copydex, are usable as stopping-out agents, but they do not stick on to the glass at all well, tending to drop away from the glass round the perimeter. Advantage of this can be taken if an area with very softly graduated edges is required, but the process is tricky.

Technique
First see that all the equipment in the aciding compound is *firm* and on an even keel. Fill the large bath up with water; then fill the smaller acid baths, as many as you think you will require, with water to the depth of 12 mm ($\frac{1}{2}$ in.), or a little less, above the ribs of the bottom. Add the acid to the water, usually one-third acid to two-thirds water. Always add the acid to the water, never the other way round. Heat is generated if the water is added to the acid depending on the proportions of the mixture; as well as driving off noxious fumes of acid, it may melt the wax stopping-out agent on the glass. Stop up the acid flask, and put it well out of the way.

Next cut small H-sections of lead from a largish calme, and set them in the acid bath, upright, so that you can read the 'H'; these should be slightly over 6 mm ($\frac{1}{4}$ in.) long, but this will vary, depending on the depth of the acid solution in the bath. The object of these little pieces of lead is two-fold. One is that they support the glass, and allow a free flow of acid solution round it; and at the same time they keep the glass away from the bottom of the bath making it fairly easy to pick up the glass by getting underneath to lift it. Dispose the lead to support the glass. There is no limit to the amount of pieces of lead in the acid bath, and in any case they gradually get eaten away, and have to be replaced.

Having stopped out the surface of the glass

where necessary, place it upside down on the lead stilts, so that the bottom face of the glass is suspended in the acid solution and the top face is free of the top of the liquid.* If this is impossible, or if the glass is going to be in the solution a long time, it may be necessary to stop out the back of the piece as well as the front. Obviously more glass exposed to the acid reduces the acid's potential, since the chemical reaction goes on over a far wider area. If acid is cheap, however, and if the glass is really thick, or if the aciding performance is only going to take a short time, it is hardly worth stopping-out the back. It is, however, extremely important to stop-out the edges of the glass all round, however tedious this performance may be. Glass that has not been stopped-out round the edges very often glazes up slack, and has to be packed. The aciding process is now well on the way, and close guard must be kept. Some glass is acided through in an instant, particularly thin flashed red, or blue, on white. As soon as the glass is acided away—which can easily be seen through the back if this has not been stopped-out (or you can lift the piece a little and have a look) it is carried straight over to the large bath of water and dumped into it. If many pieces have to be acided, you may end up with a large number of dumped pieces of glass that can be cleaned off at the end of the day. If the stopping-out agent is coming off, as much as to warrant another application, repeat the process. Replace the piece of glass with another, and so on till the end. It is as well to keep the acid-baths covered with pieces of plate glass for cleanliness, and it is usual to differentiate acid-baths of 'easy' glass, and 'stubborn' glass, with appropriately varying degrees of acid in the solution.

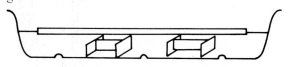

90 *H section leads supporting glass in the acid bath*

* The glass is placed aciding side downwards so that the salts formed in this process of aciding fall away from the face of the glass. If the glass were acided the other way up the salts would eventually, through building up a solid coat, inhibit the action of the acid.

Observations Generally speaking, the summer is the best time to acid. Not only is it more pleasant, but the heat in the atmosphere makes the process of aciding quicker and more even. Do not think that by greatly increasing the acid-to-water proportions the aciding will be done more quickly. If more acid is added than has been indicated, the process will certainly be quicker, but it will be far cruder at the same time. Large crystalline formations will be eaten away from the glass, leaving the flashed glass high on a plateau; this crystalline structure will be difficult to paint, and may even cause breakages in the fire. The remaining glass, in the valleys and craters, may well work out to be too thin to stand up to the ordinary handling of the glazier and cementer, and consequently will crack.

The lead blocks, as well as supporting the glass, seem to exert some kind of catalytic action on the aciding process.

Special effects of marbling can be obtained by floating Brunswick black (as bitumen paint is called in England) or Rhind's quick drying stopping-out varnish or the equivalent, on a large tub of water and, before it has hardened, gently, but firmly, placing the glass on top of the swirling random pattern; then up-turn the glass and lay aside to dry, before putting it in the acid bath as I have described.

Sometimes it is required to acid out so that a large shallow area has faded in edges. This is best done by mopping. A small ball of cotton is neatly tied to the end of a bamboo stick about 229 mm to 305 mm (9 in. to 1 ft) long, and this is dipped into the acid flask direct. (Wear rubber gloves for this operation.) Then the area is gently but persistently mopped with the neat acid. A hose with moderate flow of water on hand to cleanse the acided glass is an advantage. The mop is disposable and should be burnt as soon as operations are complete.

Cleaning out After a day or two, the acid bath will need a clean-out, owing to the large amount of salts that will have accumulated in the bottom. As these may well have quite a lot of still active acid about them they should be disposed of appropriately.

Safety precautions Hydrofluoric acid is extremely dangerous. Consequently, stringent safety precautions must be taken. I have used acid for twenty-two years or more, and the course of action I recommend is absolutely foolproof. It is quite simple. Never wear gloves or protective clothing. Roll up your sleeves and inspect your hands, to see if there are any deep little cuts on the fingers, or by the quicks; if there are, get someone else to do the job. If there are not, use the hands—quite bare—to place the glass in the acid, and to take it out; with the proviso that you must DIP THE HANDS CONSTANTLY, BETWEEN EVERY MOVEMENT IN THE ACIDING COMPOUND, INTO THE LARGE BATH OF WATER. Wash your hands with soap in cold water after a general acid session, before doing any other work. If you stick to these simple rules, there will never be any acid burns on your hands, and you will be able to handle glass in the acid bath itself without the least ill-effect. One further precaution: take the individual pieces of glass up between the thumb and forefinger, top and bottom of the glass, *not* on the edges as you would handle a clean lens, because the process of aciding sharpens any little cutting edges on the sides of the glass.

Sometimes it can be helpful to use a little metal (usually brass) pair of tongs to take the glass out of the bath and into the larger water tank. Remember two things with tongs: they may cause the glass to gyrate about the point where the tongs pick it up; they are apt to grip the glass inadequately and if the glass slips from the tongs dangerous splashes of acid may occur.

Acid burns If a burn should occur, it looks like a reddish area of irritation, perhaps with a pinprick of blood in the middle, which rapidly becomes intolerably painful and opens into an ulcer, very like a quick-lime burn. Hydrofluoric acid acts subcutaneously and is slow to begin—when started, it is usually noticed too late to arrest. Have plenty of sodium bicarbonate in powder form, and pack the wound with this until you can go to see an industrial-disease doctor; see him as soon as possible. All the acid burns I have known have happened to people who thought they were well protected and did not constantly wash their hands. One small prick in an otherwise good pair of rubber gloves will cause a great deal of trouble.

Acid can get under one's fingernails as well—but again this never occurs if one washes constantly between the slightest aciding operations.

IV *Plating*

Methods of plating, and the handling of plating, have been dealt with in the chapter on cutting. The artistic application of plating at this point of the window's development is quite common, however, and can make a very great deal of difference to the window. The only drawback to plating, apart from the technical drawback and the question of plating's durability, is that it tends to become an occupational disease, with the artist's eye always dissatisfied with the results of plating, going on making finer and finer adjustments with plating, till the whole window might resemble Jacob's ladder. There is no doubt that plating can escalate; but it is useful, not only in conjunction with aciding, but to unify a whole passage of a window that has otherwise got too thin and disparate. A single blue or green or grey can unify whole passages, if it is used in the same way as a wash would be used in painting. A flashed plating can be used to produce an effect of a patch of colour in the middle of another colour.

Having had occasion to inspect some of the windows I first did ten or twenty years ago, the plating has stood up astonishingly well to the test of time. Occasionally, however, there have been penetrations of rainwater into the space between the glasses. This is obviously avoided by cementing the two glasses together before glazing with a colourless epoxy resin.

Painting on aciding and plating

Obviously, the only surface to paint in a stained glass window is the inside surface, but choice can be made whether, in flashing, the acided side or the flat side is to be painted. It depends what you want to say. Painting on an acided surface can give a very brilliant effect, because the paint does not normally get into the valleys, and again, can be rubbed (when dry) off the protuberances with the thumb or finger.

Likewise, paint can be put on the two layers of plating independently, with a very beautiful blurred effect of double depth.

V *Enamelling*

This is the practice of putting a low-temperature coloured frit on the surface of the glass, and firing it in, at a lower temperature than paint, so that it fuses with the surface of the glass.

During the seventeenth and eighteenth centuries, the practice of enamelling came to the fore, since the glass makers of the time were more interested in copying paintings, i.e. making transparencies, rather than creating stained glass windows. There is no denying that many, if not most, of these transparencies are very beautiful on their own terms. Enamel, being easy to handle and having soft edges and a seductive range of colours, was very appropriate in conjunction with stain to make a coloured window over a ground of characterless white rectangular quarries. It is almost as though five generations of stained glass designers were fascinated by the invention shown in Raphael's fresco of the Miracle of St Peter in the Vatican apartments. But perhaps the aesthetic really derives from the vast trade in coloured tiles from Holland in the seventeenth and eighteenth centuries, where the pattern is painted sometimes wholly independently from the rhythm **of** the tile-quarries.

Unfortunately, enamels have a bad name for cracking and peeling off, the glass frit being of a different coefficient of expansion, presumably, to the parent glass to which it was stuck; and large portions of windows done in the seventeenth and eighteenth centuries have gone uncomfortably bald.

Modern research in enamels for glass has, I think, largely done away with the hazard of peeling and cracking, but the question remains as to whether, except for special purposes, enamel has any real application today. It is quite useful for giving a blush of one colour or another, but only occasionally. Moreover, the range of colours which really register as colour is very much more limited than it was, possibly as a consequence of the elimination of fugitive enamels.

Equipment

All that is needed is a palette for each enamel colour. Some finely ground enamel (supplied by wholesale glass and china painting enamel dealers) and a spatula or small palette knife—together with the special medium for enamels, and the thinner for this medium, which is made of oil of spike, and supplied by the Enamel Suppliers.

Technique

The enamel is very finely levigated and consequently is mixed very easily, like the paint, using the viscid medium in larger quantities than the gum in painting, and the thinner in smaller quantities than the water.

It is then painted on with very soft brushes, and can be whipped with a badger (which, however, soon gets fouled up). Enamel is useless where precise definition is concerned, because of its habit of spreading over the surface of the glass into an ill-defined area, and the thicker the enamel is put on, the greater the spread. Too thickly or coarsely applied enamel bunches into blobs, and never develops its colour. Enamel, owing to the high degree of fluxing agent it contains, tends to dissolve paint already applied to the glass and fired, if it gets on to it, disturbing its homogeneous quality.

VI Fused Glass Techniques

These are not to be confused with the polyester-resin techniques of bringing glass together in little bits and chips. This is the last, and the least satisfactory, method of effecting change of colour or emphasis within the boundaries of the leading. Individual pieces of glass are fused together at a very high temperature of at least 200°C higher than the normal temperature at which stained glass is fired. The pieces of glass can either be fused together in a kind of fricassée, in which case very great care has to be taken over the edges, so that they are joinable with lead; or smaller pieces of glass can be melted onto the surface of a 6 mm ($\frac{1}{4}$ in.) plate glass which has been cut to the cutline shape. The latter is the better way, no doubt, but both are liable to cracks and splits after a very short time, owing to the different coefficients of expansion of the different glasses. One has a feeling that, physically, glass of this sort is always under tension. Artistically, the effect is almost always meretricious, fussy, and inarticulate. It seems quite impossible to control an artistic statement that consists of a string of smaller artistic statements of such minuscule pointlessness, as fused-glass methods produce. If kaleidoscopic effects are really needed, the best way to produce them is in the twelfth-century method, with a lead between each tiny piece of glass; at least that way it will last.

When the first painting has been done and fired, and the second painting—the aciding and plating put into position, the staining done and fired, and any enamelling done, if it is necessary—the window may be glazed.

Firing

The stained glass kiln

There are many kinds of stained glass kilns on the
market at the moment. They are, in general,
divided up into gas and electricity, and subdivided
into open or closed.

The principle of heating the glass is exactly
the same, whether gas or electricity is used. In
each case the glass must go through the same
stage of preheating before firing, and cooling
down after having been fired, though the time
factor of these may vary. It is possible to get a
more even distribution of heat with gas, particularly in the short heating-up stage.

Gas heating

1 One type of kiln has a number of gas-jets
positioned at intervals along the side of the firing
chamber; these play up on to the roof of the
chamber, the heat being reflected downwards
towards the face of the glass. This method is not
too satisfactory from the point of view of even
heat-distribution.

2 Another type of kiln has an electrically driven
gas-and-air mix impeller. The gas and air mixture
is forced into the top of the kiln through a single
pipe, and is directed down onto, and through, a
special porous brick, which itself forms the roof
of the firing chamber. The gas is lit on the underside of the brick, starting off as a blue flame, and
rising to red as the heat builds up in the chamber.
The fire-brick roof so heated tends to be hotter
in the middle, and well below firing temperature
at the outside—with the result that the glass has

to be placed in the middle of the trays, otherwise
it does not get fired properly.

3 Another kiln has been invented by Mr Hugh
Powell, in conjunction with the Gas Board of
Great Britain. This is a modification of the last
method of heating. Four jets of gas are played in
from each side, eight in all. The roof of the firing
chamber is constructed of four sections of porous
brick in honeycomb formation. These sections
are set at an angle, towards each other, with a
ridge running from front to rear along the whole
centre line of the roof of the firing chamber.
This method avoids any hot spots in the kiln,
and ensures that every part of the kiln gets an
even heat, consequently the full extent of the
tray may be used.

Advantages of gas

The main advantage is the saving in time and
money. Gas kilns are cheaper to construct than
electric kilns, and they are quicker at heating up:
the first tray of the gas kiln described above can be
fired within twenty minutes of lighting the jets.
Gas is also more economical to run than electricity.

Gas kilns do not normally have a pyrometer or
temperature gauge attached to them, though this
can be added. All the firing is done purely by
eye, using a spy-hole in the door of the firing
chamber.

Points to note

1 Although both the previously mentioned kilns
are gas kilns, a supply of electricity is essential

to drive the electric motor which feeds the kiln with the gas and air mixture. Normally one or two-phase electricity is needed for this.

2 Make sure, when using a gas kiln, that all water and damp have been driven out of the fire brick. Gas itself has a water content when it is burnt, and this will condense on the cold glass if the gas is not sufficiently hot inside the firing chamber before introducing the glass.

3 Make sure that the door or doors to the firing chamber are well fitting, as gas, far more than electricity, is susceptible to draughts—which results in uneven firing.

Electric kilns

The open kiln Nearly all electric kilns work off three-phase electricity: and before thinking of buying a kiln you should thoroughly check your electrical supply. Changing to three-phase could materially affect the total cost of installing a kiln. This is the usual kind of electric kiln used. It consists of three parts:

(a) the rack, to hold the trays which are being fired or have been fired;
(b) the firing chamber;
(c) the annealing chamber.

As in the previous description of gas kilns, electric kilns of this type are designed to be continually fed with trays of glass, which are fired for a short time and then moved on.

1 *The firing chamber* (see figure 91b) has positions in it for two trays, one on top of the other. The trays may be moved in and out independently. The electric elements are threaded through firebrick forming the roof of the firing chamber. These are distributed all over the ceiling or at the sides of the kiln or along the length of the left- and right-hand edges of the ceiling of the firing chamber. As all the variations are designed to distribute the heat in the kiln as efficiently as possible, it is worth asking manufacturers where the elements are sited before buying. The result of inefficient siting is bad firing of the glass, occurring either round the perimeter of the tray or in the middle.

2 *The annealing chamber* (see diagram below). This is a small flat chamber immediately above the firing chamber, which is not heated, but which gets very warm from the heat of the firing chamber below. It has good insulation all round it, and a flapdown door. It takes one tray of glass at a time.

The rheostat (e) is a device with which to syphon off electricity and regulate the overall performance of the kiln by reducing the heat of the firing chamber. It is situated, most often, each side of the rack below the kiln holding the waiting

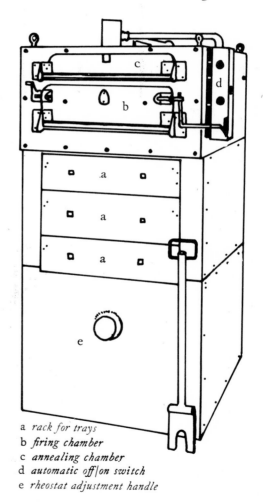

a *rack for trays*
b *firing chamber*
c *annealing chamber*
d *automatic off/on switch*
e *rheostat adjustment handle*

91　*The open electric kiln showing rheostat knob at base*
　　　a *removable doors to tray rack*

trays. When the rheostat is turned up, less heat goes to the kiln, and more is lodged in the rheostat. It is not a method of conserving electricity. In theory the rheostat is useful; in practice, owing to the electric kiln being wired up in two or three different phases, the turning up of the rheostat sometimes plays about with the phasing, thus leading to bad distribution of heat in the firing chamber.

In some kilns, particularly the closed kiln, a make-and-break system of electrical control results in a far more even and efficient temperature.

The closed kiln

This kiln is made up of one large firing chamber, exactly like a pottery kiln, with a heavy firebrick door to close it. The door has two firebrick plugs

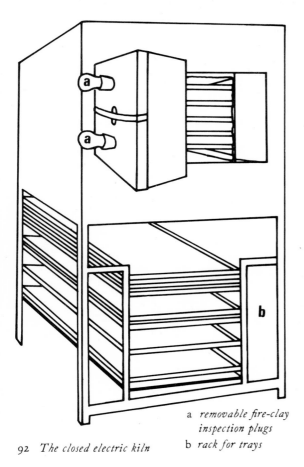

a *removable fire-clay inspection plugs*

b *rack for trays*

92　*The closed electric kiln*

which can be moved, to look at the kiln's performance. A steel rack built into the firing chamber can be designed to take several trays—about eight is the most satisfactory.

The temperature-rise of the kiln, controlled by the make-and-break mechanism, fires in one even progression. Once the glass has been laid on to trays and stacked in the kiln, the door shut, and all the controls properly set, you can in theory go out for the day wenching, and come back and find everything done. But in fact things are not as simple as that. The trays must be very carefully loaded because of the inevitably uneven distribution of heat—the hardest glass being put in the hotter places, and the softer glass where the cold spots are in the kiln.

Read carefully all the manufacturer's instructions, and have one of their representatives present to supervise the putting in of the kiln and the correct installation of all the electrical switches and adjuncts if that is at all possible.

Siting of kilns

Make certain that the kiln is in the right place to be comfortably operated by right-handed or left-handed people. A kiln in a corner is hardly ever a good idea. Make sure that the trays can be manœuvred efficiently, with nothing behind the operator to bump into, and that, in the case of an electric kiln, the annealing chamber at the top can be reached without undue heaving and stretching, and without the trays tilting or spilling their glass. A shower of glass and hot plaster on the forearms can be very painful indeed. At either side of the kiln there should be benches on which to put the trays, ready for replenishing with glass to be fired. In front of the kiln there should be a removable duckboard—large, soundly constructed, and at the right height for reaching the annealing chamber comfortably, when standing on it.

There should be a bin handy to hold the spent plaster off the trays.

The pyrometers should be properly sited so they are easy to read.

Materials of trays

All kilns have removable trays made of an angle-iron perimeter, so constructed as to hold a loose sheet of asbestos or steel. The tray slides in and out on rails in the firing chamber, and the sheet is covered with a fine layer of plaster of Paris, on which the glass actually rests.

Asbestos trays should be dried out, to begin with, by putting them in the kiln at a sub-temperature, then taking them out and turning them over so that they do not warp or buckle. They should dry out evenly on both sides. The steel trays should be broken in by heating in the firing chamber, cooling, turning over and heating again. This should remove any temper in them, and should ensure that the trays stay even and flat when firing.

Whitening, or plaster of Paris, finely ground, should be placed on the top of the trays to a depth of between 3 mm and 5 mm ($\frac{1}{8}$ in. and $\frac{3}{16}$ in.) The whitening or plaster has to be dried out in the kiln, too, to drive off any latent moisture, before it is possible to put glass on top of it. The reason for the plaster is to prevent the glass from sliding about on the tray. It also protects the tray from most of the direct heat, so lengthening its life.

Whitening has something of a suspect name in the firing of glass. I am not sure why. I have never used whitening alone; I generally use half whitening and half plaster of paris (I always prefer to use pure dental plaster of paris).

Levelling the plaster

Make certain that the plaster is level, with no bumps or depressions. Any bump or depression will show in the glass, distorting the back, if it is fired above a certain temperature.

A good way of making the plaster level is shown in the diagram. Place a strip of plate glass the exact internal width of the tray on the plaster of Paris; begin at one end, and slowly draw the strip of glass the whole length of the tray. Hold the strip between thumb and forefinger, and raise the front edge of the strip clear of the plaster. It may be necessary to go backwards and forwards in this way several times before the plaster is smooth and evenly distributed all over the tray. The plaster should not go *right* to the edge of the

tray, because as the asbestos or steel is loose (to allow for expansion all round), there is bound to be a gap through which plaster may fall, either on to newly fired glass below, spoiling the quality of the paint, or on to glass which is just going to be fired, in which case plaster gets incorporated into the paint.

You can alway scrape up the unwanted plaster round the sides with a thin spatula or knife—and finish off by brushing the remaining plaster up into the firing area and then lightly smoothing with the plate glass—but only once.

Remember, little jerks and hitches during the movement of the trays when you are handling them in and out of the kiln always dislodge small amounts of plaster.

Placing the glass on the plaster

When firing directly from the easel or plate-glass panel, which is more usual today than firing from painted glass that has been trayed, handle the glass with extra care, to make certain that the paint is not damaged or smudged in any way by tools or fingers. The best way to lever glass from wax or plasticine is to insert the point of a glazing knife actually into the plasticine, or very near to it. In this way there is no risk of breaking the glass by levering it up in the middle while the corners are still firmly attached with wax or plasticine. Get rid of any pieces of plasticine and have a damp rag handy to wipe off any drips of paint that may have dribbled down the back in the course of painting. Place the glass lightly on

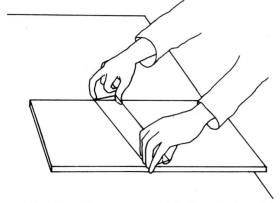

93 *Levelling plaster on tray with piece of plate glass*

the plaster, painted side uppermost, and give it a very gentle press. Do not attempt to move glass once it has been placed. Be very careful not to let one piece of glass touch another on the tray, and do not fill the tray beyond the limits that you know will give an efficient fire, which is usually 25 mm to 38 mm (1 in. to 1½ in.) from the back side of the tray; this, of course, varies with the efficiency of each kiln's performance.

Try if possible to put all soft glass on one tray, and the hard ones on another; and all the same thickness of glass together, so that there is some controllable system in firing. Obviously a thick piece of glass will require slightly more firing than a thin piece.

Handling of trays

The trays can usually be moved with the hands in loading and unloading the closed type of kiln. Owing to the heat of the trays in the *open* kiln, great care has to be taken in handling. The old way of handling is to have a lateral bracket fixed in the centre, at right angles to a wooden handle, with a circular shield of asbestos or wood to protect the hand from the heat of the tray. This bracket is held in the left hand and placed at or near the point of balance of the tray as it is taken to and from the kiln, and merely acts as a support for the dead weight of the tray. The action of dragging out the tray, guiding it, and steadying it is performed by another tool held in the right hand—a kind of universal hook which on one face acts as a drag, and on the other, when turned over, as a firm holder to the end of the tray.

The disadvantage of this handling system is that the left forearm is always under the hot tray, with the possibility of an accident, which is increased as the tray increases in size and weight.

I use a one-handed tool which does both the

94 *The handle for the kiln trays with modification shown in dotted lines*

job of supporting and of guiding. It has a very much longer metal handle, with which to get a purchase with the shoulder and elbow. This is far easier and safer to use than the two tools. The hot tray, moreover, can be kept well away from the body.

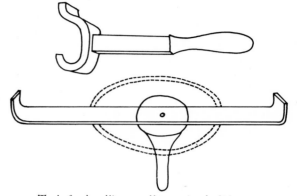

95 *Tools for handling small trays in the kiln*

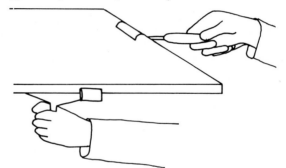

96 *Handling trays in and out of kiln*

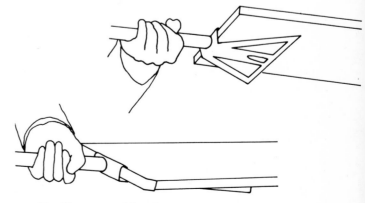

97 *Handling trays with tools*

Closed kiln firing

In the closed kiln, when the trays of glass have been loaded into the firing chamber, close the door and seal round with a thin piece of asbestos rope. Be sure that there is a good circulation of heat in and out of the trays all round the firing chamber and raise the heat very slowly. Because the kiln retains its heat very efficiently and because it will, in the course of the long pre-heating period, have built up a considerable storage of heat, it will not be necessary to raise the temperature quite as high as for an open kiln. For example, an open kiln fires the pigment at about 650°C. In the closed kiln, the temperature will only have to be raised to about 450° to 480°C, and it should hold this temperature for about four hours.

Should the temperature be raised in the closed kiln as high as 600°C, or 650°C, you will find that the majority of the glass will be over-fired and spoilt; in fact, it may have melted and be blistered beyond recovery.

If the temperature is raised too quickly, this will result in uneven firing. The lower trays in the kiln will be fired hard, or boiled, while the trays at the top will be unfired. When the glass has been successfully fired, which can only be learnt in the course of experiment and experience, switch off the kiln and allow to cool over a period of 12 to 19 hours. Then open the kiln and remove the glass.

The advantage of closed firing is that the attendance is minimal, and the area of glass fired at any one time is considerable. Just be certain that you do obtain the right type of kiln.

Open kiln firing

Having loaded the trays and put them by hand into the rack provided for them underneath the kiln, switch on the kiln and put the first tray in the firing chamber on the lower of the two places whilst it is nearly cold, without a baffle to protect it.

The *baffle* is merely a spare tray with metal instead of asbestos, not covered with plaster. The baffle serves to mitigate the direct heat of the elements and protects the glass underneath from too much heat to begin with. It is naturally always put in the higher position in the firing chamber.

Put the next tray to be fired in the annealing chamber, so that it can be pre-heated slightly; this will cut down the risk of the glass bursting in the firing chamber, through being heated too quickly.

Remove the baffle and expose the glass underneath to the electrical elements, firing at 620°–630°C for 5–7 minutes.

When the tray in the kiln is fired, put the baffle in on the top position again, take out the *fired tray* (having first put the tray from the annealing chamber temporarily in the first shelf of the pre-heating rack underneath), and put it in the annealing chamber. From then on, the rhythm is quite simple:

1 Annealed tray to pre-heating rack.
2 Baffle into top position.
3 Withdrawal of fired tray and re-positioning in annealing chamber.
4 Pre-heated tray into firing chamber under baffle.
5 Wait a few minutes.
6 Withdraw baffle.
And back to 1.

The reason for the baffle technique is that the heat distribution in the firing chamber is uneven. If the glass is fired on the lower level, being farther from the elements with more room for the heated air to circulate, there is more likelihood of its getting evenly fired. When the pigment has been fired, the baffle is put back, and this takes away the direct heat and the action of firing effectively stops.

An alternative method A simpler method of firing with the same kiln abandons the use of the baffle altogether.

This consists of using both tray positions in the firing chamber. The top position will do the actual firing, being near the heated elements, whilst the position below is used as a pre-heating chamber—the tray underneath being shielded by the one that is actually being fired. When the firing has been done, the top tray is transferred to the previously vacated annealing chamber and the tray that was under it is transferred to the top position, with a fresh tray put underneath to preheat before it, in turn, is fired.

This system is admirably simple and is, in fact, what most kilns are theoretically capable of doing. It is, however, important to get a good heat over the whole surface of the top tray before it is a success. The baffle system has been found, in the circumstances, to be as near foolproof as possible. *Annealing chambers* are, though not essential, advisable, as the glass should be carefully cooled to take the temper out of it. Glass that is not carefully cooled is always liable:

1 to crack when fired a second time;
2 to crack when being cemented;
3 to crack if it has to be grozed in the course of being glazed; and finally
4 is liable to crack, quite unaccountably, after cementing when it is waiting to be put in position; these arbitrary cracks are known as cementing cracks, and are utterly infuriating because it is impossible to predict them.

Order of trays It is best to load trays to be fired into the pre-heating rack in alternate positions. These positions on the rack should be marked by a cross at the side, or by red paint. In this way eventually there will be a two-way traffic of ascending and descending trays of glass, the descending ones heating the ascending ones, and the ascending ones helping to cool the descending ones.

Cooling It is usually reckoned that the first 100°C are the most important from the point of view of correct cooling, and of those, the first 20° are most vital. Therefore the less delay between the firing chamber and the annealing chamber, the better.

Temperature of the kiln and visual appearance
Though nearly everyone has pyrometers and works from them, it is essential to know what the glass looks like at certain temperatures. This is difficult, as there are many factors involved. It depends, among other things, on how long glass has been in the kiln, and how long it has been held at certain temperatures. But for example, in a kiln gradually heating up, this is what occurs.

At 400°C the glass will not show any colour at all except at the very edges, where it will begin to glow slightly red.

At 500°C the glass looks a dull red, and is inclined to take up any irregularities in the plaster bed below it. Glass placed on the side of the bed of plaster droops down where the plaster ends. The glass paint at this stage will still look grey and flat.

At 600°C the glass paint starts to change slightly and there is a hint of a gloss on the surface of it. The glass will look a dull red, and if this temperature is held for fifteen minutes or more on glass that is thicker, you will get a very good quality in the firing of the glass. You will notice a contrast between the semi-gloss of the paint surface and the high gloss of the unpainted glass.

If you take the tray out of the kiln and hold it at eye level and look across it, you will see the light reflect off the paint. This is a successful firing. Care should be taken whilst you do this, however, to see that there are no doors or windows open near the kiln, otherwise a sudden draught could cause the glass to crack through too rapid a change of temperature.

At 650°C the glass will look a bright red. If the glass is kept in the firing chamber for longer than five to six minutes at this temperature, it will begin to distort, and the edges will lose their sharpness and become rounded; the longer you leave it, the worse it becomes—the paint will lose its crispness and the heat will draw the centres of the thinner pieces of glass towards the roof of the firing chamber, making them into shapes like bowler hats; the glass is said, at this stage, to have 'boiled'.

At 650°C, if one piece of glass is touching another, they will start to melt and fuse together.

At 700°C the glass looks a very bright red and, if touched, you find it is in a soft and putty-like state.

At 800°C the glass is well and truly at melting-point, and will be fused together. All the paint will have been distorted and become as indistinct as Roland's cry at Roncevalles.

Further rise in the temperature of the kiln will result in the sagging of the tray and its supports, and the rupture of the electrical elements.

If you have trouble remembering the kiln because you are working on your own, it might be as well to connect a parallel electrical wire to a red light that goes on over where you principally work or where the telephone or main studio door is (for going out to a midday meal for instance). Particularly when the kiln is in another room, the risk of keeping it on for too long with consequent ruin is considerable.

The art of firing

When firing glass, it is advisable to raise the temperature of the kiln to 400° or 450°C. Once that temperature has been reached, the glass itself is getting to the stage where it is beginning to fuse together with the paint. Because of this, the next stage in the firing is better carried out slowly; the slower the heat is raised, the more even the firing over the whole tray. But nowadays, when time and cost and labour have to be taken into account, it is very difficult to stick to this counsel of perfection.

If the temperature of the firing chamber is kept at an even 600°C, and the glass is fired over a fifteen-to-twelve-minute interval, it will result in a far better quality than, say, firing the glass at 650°C for only five to six minutes. The lower-temperature firing is possible owing to the cooling effect that the introduction of a fresh tray has on the firing chamber.

Timing

Only patient observation and experience will help with the exact timing of the glass in the kiln, but while the glass is pre-heating under a baffle in the firing chamber, it is useful to set a kitchen clockwork timer, so that other jobs—such as puttying, re-laying trays, or preparing stain—can be done, and time will not be wasted watching the kiln. Again, the exact length of time to set the timer is really a matter of experience. If set at five-minute intervals at first, it will serve as a rough gauge on the speed of the whole firing process. The kiln naturally heats up in the course of the day, and so the time intervals get shorter.

Faults in firing

When the glass is fired correctly, the paint should not be matt and dull, not should it be highly polished. Matt and dull paint looks horrid, even though it may be quite well fired and stable, but it catches the cement after leading up the glass, and becomes far darker and more matt. Highly polished paint looks attractive in the hand, but usually is not so good when you look through it. It loses character completely.

Over-firing is recognised immediately by the glass appearing too glossy in the fire, and the sides of the glass beginning to melt.

Re-firing *matt* glass is quite all right, and should be done, but the best thing to do with *over-fired* glass, if it has not gone too far, is to re-paint and re-fire it. If it *has* gone too far, then re-cut altogether.

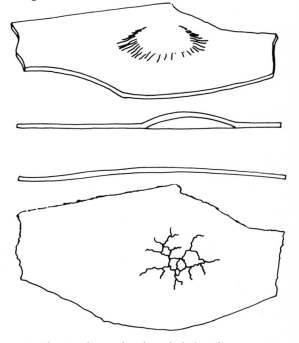

98 *Showing distorted and cracked glass due to overfiring*

The Tribe of Joseph window, Jerusalem, by Marc Chagall
Copyright ADGPA, Paris, 1977   Photograph Palphot Ltd, 1977

One of twenty windows by Brian Clarke
for Longridge Parish Church

Breakages

Glass breakages in the kiln, commonly known as fire cracks, are due to one of two things:

1. The main cause is that the glass has been badly annealed in the process of manufacture. Some indication of this will be revealed in the actual cutting of the glass. During cutting, any glass that flies apart at the first contact of the cutter should be very carefully watched when firing, and it must be very carefully heated up.
2. Another cause is that the glass has been heated up too rapidly. Thick pieces of glass, uneven pieces such as Norman Slab, pieces that have been in the acid-bath and are consequently uneven, or pieces cut from the heavier lip of an antique, all need a great deal of attention.

Two kinds of breaks

There are only two kinds of breaks in the kiln—one considerably more annoying and dramatic than the other:

1. The star crack, which is really an explosion and makes the glass fly over its neighbours, sitting on top of them and displacing them. This crack is developed during the process of heating up usually owing to too sudden violent heating. It can arise from inherent imperfections in the glass, such as soda-nuggets or small stones.
2. The cooling crack is usually a simple crack, the glass having parted, jerked apart, and the two pieces resting 2 mm to 0·79 mm ($\frac{1}{16}$ in. to $\frac{1}{32}$ in.) apart from each other. The crack is often in the shape of a symmetrical sinuous curve. Sometimes, but not often, there are subsidiary cracks behaving in the same way.

If the glass has broken in the course of cooling, it is due to one or both of two things. It has not been left long enough in the annealing chamber, and/or during its move from the firing chamber to the annealing chamber, it has been chilled by a draught. Be careful to avoid draughts in the kiln room.

Blistered paint

Paint faults that develop in the kiln are never due to the behaviour or characteristics of the glass.

They are always due to the bad mixing, handling, or painting of the pigment. Too much *gum* in the paint will cause blistering.

If the paint is put on too thickly or if it is badly mixed, it may crack and draw together in the first firing. If too much water has been used in putting the paint on thickly and darkly, it may crack.

If a particular passage is required to be dark, it is better to effect this by painting, firing, and then re-painting.

The remedy for blisters, pinholing, and for milder cracks, is to rub in raw powdered glass paint without water or gum, with your thumb, over the areas where the faults occur, and then re-fire. If the blistering is too bad, and if you cannot re-cut the glass, you may put the glass in an acid solution, weaker than is used for etching glass. All the paint will drop away in five minutes. Wash, dry, and re-paint the glass. After acid treatment however the glass never looks quite as fresh.

Disappearance of paintwork

This is a common fault, due to over-firing, but it can happen with the best firing. As Christopher Whall says in his delightful manual on stained glass 'when you first take the glass out of the kiln you wish you had never been born'. Glass that was crisply painted has run and gone transparent. All the delicate transparencies and mattes completely vanished. Re-painting is the only remedy. Curiously enough, the paint does not lose its virtue and character nearly so much on the second firing.

Behaviour of glass in the kiln

Some of the different glass that is used in stained glass behave very singularly in the fire.

Reds Some *flashed rubies*, particularly if the flash is thin or salmon colour, tend to go pale in the first fire and come back to normal colour in subsequent firings. Others go pale and stay pale. Others start pale and develop into a full-bodied red.

Selenium reds, as a rule, change to an unpleasant marmalade colour or bright orange. Since this change is almost unavoidable, however lightly it is fired, the best thing to do is to plate the selenium with a thin piece of white glass. Paint the white glass and fire it carefully, so that—in common with all fired plating—it is flat and easy to lead up afterwards, and put it back on the selenium red.

Blues Some Prussian blues and many *greens* sulphur in the fire. This is usually confined to flashed glass in the blues, but any bottle green tends to sulphur. This is a curious, unpleasant scum, like a metallic film on the surface of the glass, where it has not been painted. It is quite fixed against ordinary means of cleaning, but is removed easily by wiping with acid. Avoid getting the acid on the paint, as it will be destroyed instantly.

Yellows tend, if they are cadmium yellows, to lose the brightness of their colour, particularly the lemon yellows.

All other colours are unaffected by heat, but certain colours have physical reactions to the fire. *Flashed glasses* tend to shrink and distort at a far lower temperature than ordinary pot glass.

Flashed glasses that have been acided and *painted*, should be fired with extra care because of the different thicknesses in the same piece, and the consequent stresses in the glass.

99 *The Trinity window in Stretford Parish Church, Manchester. Designed and executed by Geoffrey Clarke 1961*

100 *Nôtre Dame du Raincy, outside Paris, c 1922.*
   Auguste Perret, architect
   Marguerite Huré, stained glass artist

Staining Glass

First make a stain reference device (see page oo) so that you may readily see the way in which the glass you may wish to stain will behave.

It should also be a general craft discipline towards the end of the firing day, when the kiln is cooling down, to fire samples of any new glass you have just been cutting. These should be stain-sampled first to see if they react. Obviously if the samples do not work it may pay to re-cut them in glass that *will* take stain before you bother to paint your window. This will save time and disappointment.

Do not forget to stain on the reverse side to the paint.

Mixing the stain

Mix the stain in either of the two ways described on pages 79–80, so that it becomes a smooth, thick paste. Dilute with as much water as necessary when actually staining.

When applying stain make sure you keep it thoroughly mixed, especially if you are using a weak stain. The stain and the water tend to separate out, leaving an uneven and blotchy effect on the glass.

Firing stain

The best results, and the most predictable ones, come from firing stain at a low temperature. The best time to do this is at the end of the firing day, when the kiln has been switched off or about to be switched off and there is a long-lasting, but slowly declining heat. The best heat for a stain is what is known as a soaking fire rather than a firm, short fire. Never fire stain at the same time as pigment unless the very darkest results are required. The advantage of firing stain in a diminishing heat is that if by mistake it is left in the firing chamber too long, the chance of any damage being done is progressively diminished as time goes on. But at the same time, the length of time needed to stain gets materially longer.

Here is a rough guide as to what happens in the kiln to individual colours when stained.

Yellow The majority of yellow glasses stain well. Very deep ambers and yellows can be obtained on all French yellows. English yellows tend to be disappointing.

Whites English whites are very hard and the stain needs to be put on rather thickly and fired for a longer time than usual. The greener the white is, the easier it is to stain, but the result may be unpleasant. English *Reamy* whites are very susceptible to stain and will stain easily at a very low temperature.*

* If you have seen the Baptistry window in Coventry Cathedral which we made, you will see that the centre of this is entirely composed of *stained* glass. For this we used very pale yellows, rose, and white glass. This staining had to be done very carefully, and very slowly owing to the glass being so sensitive. It was fired at a temperature of 500°C for a time of three to four minutes for the pale stain, and for a little longer for the deeper ones.

Another example of a very complex and delicate stained window we have made is at St Woolo's Cathedral in Newport, Monmouthshire, South Wales.

French whites and some *German whites* stain very beautifully indeed in the whole range of stain from lightest daffodil yellow to the most sonorous amber. But on the other hand some German whites are disappointing and hardly stain at all.

German opaque glasses and opalescent glasses should not, in my opinion, be stained at all.
Greens English greens, in the majority, are very stubborn to stain. Only the very palest greens or the flash greens stain successfully and these can be very subtle. French greens are rather better in this respect.
Blues Many blues stain very readily and a series of the most beautiful and delicate greens can be produced depending on the strength of the stain and the depth of the blue. English blues will stain well on the whole—but the more attractive and deeper cobalt they become, the more difficult it is to stain them. English staining blue, made specially for the purpose, is justly famous for the beauty of the greens it produces.

Obviously it is possible to work the changes between flashed blue where the acided portions are worked in counterpoint to the stained portions, i.e. you can vary the stain and the colour—and have a very *heavy* stain over light acided blue and very *light* stain over light acided blue, and very dark blue all on the same piece of glass.

English flashed blue stains well on both blue and flashed sides.

French blue stains well when mid-tinted—not so well when pale, usually rather a weak lemon, and not so well when dark. French blues can be made to yield a crushed mulberry colour with heavy firing.

German blues do not stain well on the whole.
Reds Reds will stain well on the white side. Stain on the flash red side may drive out the red or the salmon and substitute yellow.

All flashed glass should be stain sampled on both sides, before cutting, in case the cutting should have to be reversed.

Faults in staining

If the stain is fired too long it will be too dark, and will be covered with a permanent opaque green scum on the stained side, known as metal-ling. Metalling dulls the yellow and makes it go muddy. This is a very common occurrence when any amount of stain has to be applied, and is one of the reasons why stain is applied to the outer surface of the glass. Metalling on the outside of a building is ugly enough, as can often be seen, particularly in late nineteenth century windows in England, but on the inside of a building looks extremely unattractive in back lighting.

If by mistake metalling does occur, it can generally be removed by carefully mopping with hydrofluoric acid (see section on Aciding, page 81) but make sure that the paint is protected on the other side, so that the acid cannot touch this and destroy it. Waxing the paint is a good precaution—a small paraffin (kerosene) bath gets rid of the wax afterwards.

Sometimes stain on the white part of red glass that has been acided, comes out very reluctantly and sourly. The remedy for this is to acid the red in two stages. Stop out all the passages needed to be red first and acid until all the red on the intended white areas is turned very light salmon colour. Then withdraw the piece from the acid bath, dry it thoroughly, and re-wax where you wish to stain as well as the original red areas. The rest of the red glass is now acided white. You have as a result one piece of glass with areas of red salmon and white. So the final result will be to obtain red, yellow and white on the same pieces of glass, the yellow being the salmon red passages which have been stained.

Additional technique

Staining can of course be used in conjunction with aciding and plating, to produce the most complex effects. Two or three different weights of stain can be applied on one piece of glass if the firing is done in various stages. Simply apply stain on what is to be the dark area first, and fire it fairly lightly—then apply the stain over the passage which is going to be light, and fire lightly again when the new stain will turn lemon yellow and the old stain will darken to amber. When you know your glass and your stain well, you will be able to get any number of nuances of stain together on the same piece of glass.

Enamelling

Enamel (see page 87) is fired at a little above the temperature of stain. Though enamels are better than they were, they are still not very reliable and of course have a limited colour range. Pale green on blue glass can be very beautiful; cherry reds and carmines are also effective.

It is better to do a separate firing for enamel *before* the stain fire if the enamel and the stain are both on the same piece of glass. The enamel requires a rather longer time in the kiln than stain does, but still far below the time needed for paint. The subtlety of the change of colour that can be effected with enamels is very wide (it really acts as a kind of plating), but it will depend a lot on the firing of the enamel, because the longer enamel is fired the more it changes colour. Here again a series of experiments and detailed samples will help you get to know how the enamel behaves on certain colours and you can plan your effects ahead.

Since enamel is a fairly free-flowing frit applied to the glass it has the advantages and disadvantages of this fact. Having a high proportion of flux in it, it tends to dissolve the paint with which it comes into contact. Again in the course of firing, enamel seems more susceptible than any other medium to spoiling by being accidentally powdered over with plaster of paris in the course of firing. Once this happens it is virtually impossible to do anything about it: it looks very unsightly.

General Thoughts on Firing and Kilns

When choosing a kiln think of who is going to use it, and the kind of work for which it is to be used. If women and girls are expected to use it, have a kiln with trays which they can lift and move about easily. Otherwise they are unfairly restricted in learning by not being able to do their own firing.

Some electric kilns are not well designed. The fittings of some kilns are not well finished either. In many kilns, even the best, unless very carefully handled, things will bend and nuts and bolts will be lost. Doors of kilns can be particularly troublesome.

Be careful in a closed kiln that the iron tray frame is not made too close to the tray rails. The heat may not be able to circulate well, and there may be a lot of shaling from the metal which will spoil the glass.

The open kiln, for those who like to fire each piece of glass carefully and give it every attention, is still the best one. The idea of putting a piece of glass as large as 60 sq cm (2 sq ft) in the kiln would formerly have been quite unheard of, however, with a modern kiln, provided the trays are large enough and the firing chamber well insulated, this can be done easily. The glass must merely be heated and cooled very slowly.

Technique of Glazing

The glazing bench

If there is enough space available, the ideal thing is to have a room set aside exclusively for glazing. Whether you have this or not, the following multi-purpose glazing bench is essential. Its basic measurement should be 3·6 m × 1·8 m (12 ft × 6 ft). However, since there are occasions when the work done demands extra width of working space, it may be an advantage to have a fairly broad flap running down one side of the bench, to be put up or down as the occasion demands. Underneath the bench, which should be not *more* than 100 cm (40 in.), and not *less* than 76 cm (30 in.) in height, is a very useful storage space; it can be divided into three sections: one for trays, another (the largest) for storing upright the panels already glazed and ready for cementing, and the third for the plate-glass panels from which the antique painted glass has, for the time being, been removed. The space underneath can also be used for storing lead but in this case you should adopt the method of having the lead calmes in separate troughs, or coffins, on rollers, so that they can be pulled out from the end of the glazing bench (otherwise a lot of the interior space is wasted). Lastly, it is both useful and convenient for a series of drawers to be fitted under the bench, to the right-hand side (assuming right-handedness) so that the hand can automatically go to the right drawer to get out any of the many different tools and odd materials that are needed in glazing.

The storage of trays in the bench, which are intended to take the fired glass, laid out neatly in the correct order for glazing, are necessary from any point of view. After the final painting and staining, when the glass is taken from the plate glass for the last time and cleaned up, it is laid in order on the trays, ready for glazing. If more than one layer of glass is put in a tray, then a piece of newspaper is put between the various layers of glass. The only things to make sure of in doing this are: (1) that the glass to be leaded is in the right pane order; generally speaking since one glazes from the bottom of a window towards the top, the glass that has been fired for the top of the window should go on the tray first, as it will eventually end up being the last glass to be fired. (2) that no very great quantity of the glass to be leaded is missing, (being re-fired or stained) because it will be impossible to introduce it into a series of layers of glass which are already stored away on the trays, without producing complete chaos.

If it is not feasible to store lead under the bench, then the best rack to make is one that has a series of angle-iron supports coming out of the wall, and firmly attached to the wall, which will support troughs or coffins of lead calmes. These should be of the appropriate dimensions for the lead you are likely to be using.

There is a case, especially in a small studio, for having all other working surfaces portable, so that they can be set up on trestles when and where needed, but in the case of the workbench for glazing the more fixed and solid it is the better.

Glazing benches must have a good overhead

light or should face the window. Nothing is more annoying than working in one's own light.

A system of calor or propane gas pipes, with nipples placed at convenient points, is extremely useful. Gas soldering is always preferable to electric soldering (see page 118), and the inconvenience of lugging a large bottle of gas from glazing bench to glazing bench can well be imagined. The expense of laying on a gas supply is amply repaid, but the important thing to remember is that the nipples must never be low down on the far side of the bench (as in a chemical laboratory), otherwise the high-pressure gas piping, from the nipple to the handle of the soldering-iron, will always be in the way. The permanent gas nipple should be well overhead, on a line just behind the shoulders of the glazier as he bends over the bench, and there should be sufficient length of gas tubing to drape the floor and come up to the hand holding the soldering-iron. The soldering-iron should always be laid down (at half-heat) on a rest made of iron for this purpose, either on the bench or well overhead, but away from anything inflammable.

On no account lean the soldering-iron, whilst still alight, near the glazing, the cutline, or the tallow. Do not forget that propane gas is heavier than air, and that if the soldering-iron is turned on and not lit, the act of lighting—owing to the accumulation of gas—will turn the whole bench, and sometimes the glazier, into a considerable Christmas pudding.

It is an invariable rule in my studio to turn the calor gas off at the main every evening.

A *duck-board* to stand on whilst glazing is a good idea.

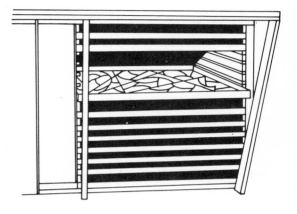

102 *Glazing bench showing pieces of glass laid out on tray*

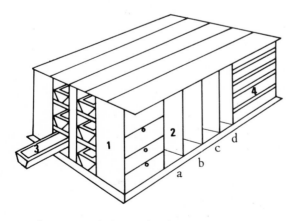

101 *Large central glazing bench*
  1 *drawers*   3 *lead storage*
  2 *racks*   4 *tray racks*

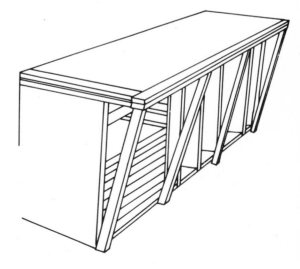

103 *Simple glazing bench*

104

104 *Detail of windows in the August Pieperhaus,*
Aaachen, Germany, designed by Ludwig Schaffrath

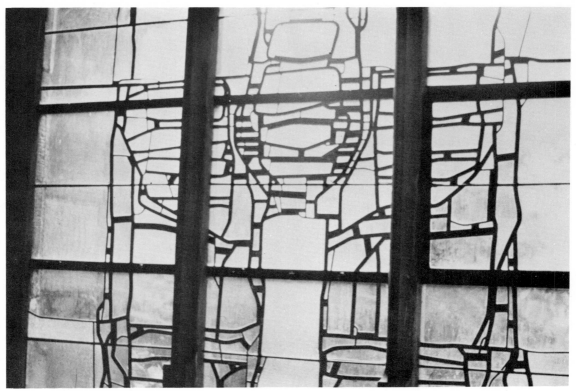

105 *Detail of cloister window, Aachen Cathedral, designed by Ludwig Schaffrath*

106 *Detail of window, one of a series by Jacques Villon, executed by Charles Marq 1957–8 for Metz Cathedral, showing the sophisticated use of leading and glass*

107 *Detail of East window, Priesterhaus Maria Rast,*
designed by Ludwig Schaffrath

108 *Window in a church north of Zurich, Switzerland.*
Designed by Ferdinand Gehr 1962, showing use of
unpainted glass in lead calmes. The scale is con-
siderable as can be seen from the chairs

Tools

There is, unfortunately, no list of glazier's tools as such. All the tools that a glazier uses are ones that he has adapted for the job.

Two may be classed as his tools and these are the glass cutter and glass pliers. There is also a stopping knife, which is made from an oyster knife with a lump of lead moulded on to the end of the handle to be used for tapping the glass and for knocking in the nails. The *stopping knife* end is used for glazing, i.e. actually manipulating the lead into the correct position and the lead end as a gentle kind of hammer. The *cutting knife* is a square-ended, good steel knife, and this is best made from a putty knife with the end which was originally angled, ground off square. When you are choosing a cutting knife it is best to *avoid* one that has the steel running through the handle. The continental or German lead-cutting knife is shaped very much like a linoleum-cutting knife, with the distinction that it is sharpened on the outside of the blade. The action of cutting the lead is effected by gently rolling the knife forward and down onto the lead. You hold the knife handle rather in the manner you would in stabbing a shark: the action, however, is far gentler. You will need a good *steel square*, a good *straight-edge*, a pair of ordinary *pliers* with side cutters and a side guillotine on the edge, a pair of *pincers*, a *lathekin* which is generally shaped by the craftsman out of a piece of boxwood or bone. You will require an *oilstone, a rule, and a soldering-iron.* Electric soldering-irons are not really very much use for this work, as it is very difficult to control their heat. *Gas*, on the other hand, is very suitable, either bottled or from the mains, but you must ensure that you have the right sized jet for the right type of gas. The *solder* you use is commonly called blowpipe solder, and is best bought in thin strips rather than thick heavy ones.

Glazing

Though the materials have changed in size and shape and texture, the actual process of glazing, or leading glass, has not changed at all from the time it was first done.

The first operation is to pin the cutline to the glazing-bench. If it is going to have a straight edge, trim the cutline to the straight side of the panel, that is, the glass-cutting side.

Then pin it to the bench. The distance of the straight-edge line (marked on the cutline) from the lath running along the near side of the glazing bench is governed by the size of the rebate into which the panel is finally to be fixed *on site*. If it is going into stonework, the normal depth of the rebate, or groove in the stonework, is $\frac{3}{8}$ in. or rebate, or groove in the stonework, is 9 mm or 12 mm ($\frac{3}{8}$ in. or $\frac{1}{2}$ in.). Therefore all that is needed is a 12 mm ($\frac{1}{2}$ in.) outside lead.

You will find that different ages of building have different methods of seating.

Twelfth, thirteenth and fourteenth centuries: grooves
Fifteenth and sixteenth centuries: rebates
Nineteenth century: grooves
Twentieth century: more often than not, rebates

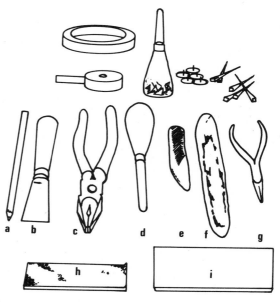

109 *Glazing tools*
  a *chinagraph pencil*   f *large lathekin*
  b *knife*   g *small pliers*
  c *pliers*   h *hone tone*
  d *oyster knife*   i *carborundum*
  e *lathekin*

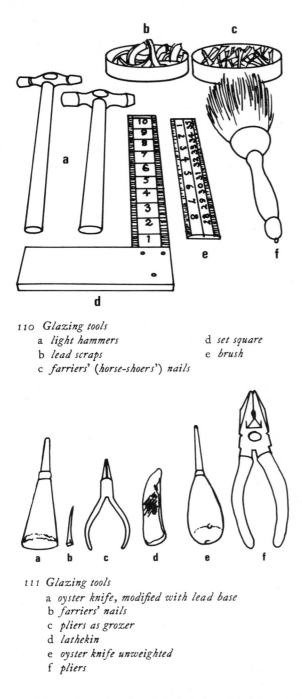

110 *Glazing tools*
  a *light hammers*   d *set square*
  b *lead scraps*   e *brush*
  c *farriers' (horse-shoers') nails*

111 *Glazing tools*
  a *oyster knife, modified with lead base*
  b *farriers' nails*
  c *pliers as grozer*
  d *lathekin*
  e *oyster knife unweighted*
  f *pliers*

If, on the other hand, it is being fixed into a metal or wooden frame, the depth and width of the rebate must be found out first. You must allow for 3 mm ($\frac{1}{8}$ in.) strip of lead to show between the actual glass and the stonework. This is because, when the panel is bedded and glazed into its frame, if this 3 mm ($\frac{1}{8}$ in.) is allowed for it will make a far better and more waterproof seal between the stone and the glass, than if the lead is pushed completely into the rebate. It will look better artistically too.

Though border-leads can be 15 mm ($\frac{5}{8}$ in.) (indeed, they can be any width, within reason, beyond 12 mm ($\frac{1}{2}$ in.)), for the sake of the description following, the normal width of 12 mm ($\frac{1}{2}$ in.) for the border-lead is taken for granted.

Working on the assumption that a 12 mm ($\frac{1}{2}$ in.) lead is being used, the cutline is pinned on to the bench with the side line 6 mm ($\frac{1}{4}$ in.) away from the lath. This will mean that the *sight-size* of the panel will be the right distance away from the lath; and that the *glass-size* will run (unseen) just inside the cutline perimeter. The measurements of the placing of the cutline to the lath may be checked all along the line, by means of a little sample (say 50 mm (2 in.)) of the outside lead that is going to be used.

The next thing to do is to select the lead you will use. Do not take too much, but there again, do not take too little: getting one calme at a time means an endless jog-trot through the studio, disturbing the rhythm of the work. Get two or three calmes of each size to be used and at the same time check up in the glazier's shop as to whether there are any convenient left-over leads from previous work which could be used.

It goes without saying that it is artistically ridiculous to use leads of a different character in any one piece of work: apart from the lap-leads and the edge-leads, which are always flat for ease of manipulation, the mixing of round, beaded, and/or flat leads in a panel is banal artistically and unprofessional from the point of view of craft. Whereas in England the round-leaf lead is always used for work on the interior of a panel, and beaded or flat lead is always used as outside perimeter lead, in Germany elegant beaded lead is used all the time. This imports a great sense of style to German glazing which is undoubtedly the best standard of glazing in the world.

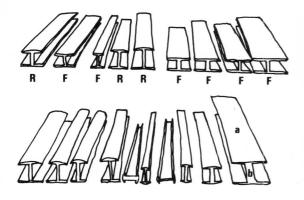

112 *Various sections of lead. Note differences of heart and leaf*
   R *round*   F *flat*

Stretching the lead

The lead must be stretched before it is used in glazing. This not only corrects any faults, such as wobbles, bends, and kinks which may be a result of bad handling, having been twisted when put into the racks or bruised by other lead when being pulled out roughly, but it does something to strengthen and toughen the lead itself, and makes it easier to handle, and firmer under the cutting knife.

Stretching lead is done by inserting one end of the calme (possibly folded back on itself for 50 mm (2 in.)) into the lead-vice, and gripping the other firmly in a pair of pliers. The second end of the calme, particularly if it is thin, can be turned in on itself, too, to give more grip to the pliers. Pull the lead out quite straight, turning the pliers one way or another, if it is called for, to straighten out any barley-sugar twist there may be in the calme.

The best way of stretching the lead is first of all to take the slack, holding one hand flat on top of the hand holding the pliers, and—making sure that one foot is out behind the other one—rock firmly back, using the front foot to push your weight backwards. The leg at the back will save you from losing balance if the lead should break owing to a flaw or it slipping out of the lead vice.

Then carefully carry the lead to the bench, and lay it well clear of the work.

113 *Detail of window by Anton Wendling*

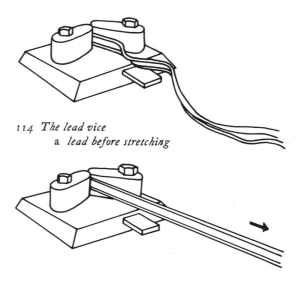

114 *The lead vice*
   a *lead before stretching*

b *lead after stretching*

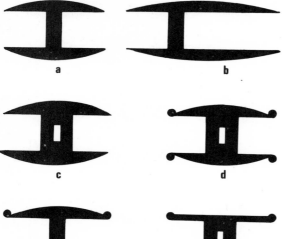

115 *Different sections of lead*
    a *round*   e *filleted*
    b *round eccentric*   f *flat steel core*
    c *round steel core*   g *flat*
    d *filleted steel core* h *flat eccentric*

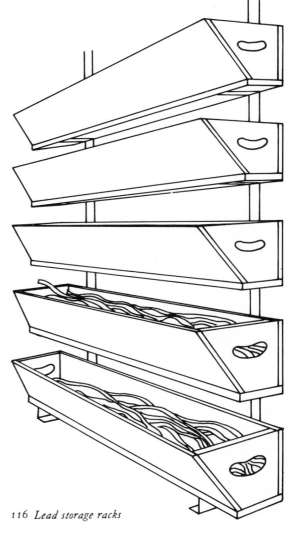

116 *Lead storage racks*

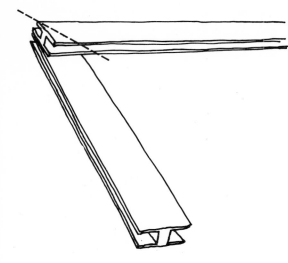

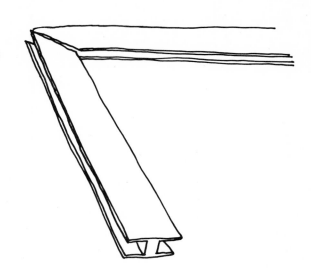

117 *Placing of lead before cutting mitre*
   a *mitre line*

118 *After cutting mitre*

Mitring corners

It is assumed that two 12 mm ($\frac{1}{2}$ in.) wide strips of border-lead have been cut to the desired length, and laid on the bench against the laths, at right angles to one another, so as to form a side and a bottom line of a panel. If this panel is eventually going into stonework, the corners of the outside lead will have to be mitred.

The method of doing this is to lay the side lead abutting fully to the base lath; and the base lead abutting fully to the side lath (so that their ends are squarely on top of each other), and make a 45° cut down through the two leads simultaneously. This will ensure that the mitre joint fits and matches perfectly.

If the panel is being glazed into a wood or metal frame, there is no need to mitre the corners. Cut the leads square on, but lay the vertical border-lead the full length of the panel, and abut the base lead on to it, so that the finished panel has two vertical border-leads leading right down to the base-line.

Before putting the border-lead in its position, and fixing it there temporarily with farrier's nails, it is best to open the lead a little on both

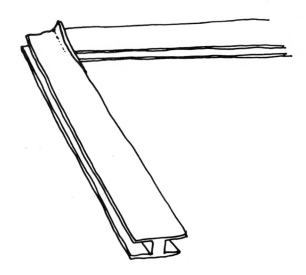

119 *Abutting the outer lead at a corner*

sides with the lathekin. This enables the lead to stand up to pressure against the lath, under which it might otherwise fold up, and allows the glass and the subsidiary lead of the panel to fit snugly without faults into, and under, the lip of the outside lead.

The lathekin

The lathekin is usually handmade by the craftsman to suit his own hand, and is very much a personal tool or instrument. It can be made from box-wood or bone, each being hard, and can be finished off smoothly. It is shaped and curved to fit the hand with one end pointed and narrow, gradually widening to the other, less pointed end as shown in the sketch.

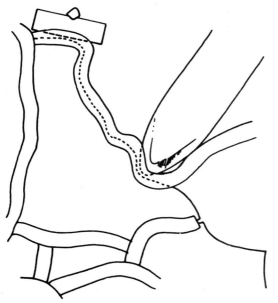

120 *Method of using the lathekin*

The lathekin is used in the process of glazing initially to widen out the flat outside lead so that the glass will fit into it easily. It is also used when working an inside lead into a tight curve, being used to bring pressure to bear on the heart of the lead—not the leaf.

121 *Opening the lead with the lathekin*

When you take your glass out from the tray on which it has been laid, check it, to see if any bits are lost; and clean it, removing dust, glass chips, pieces of plasticine, and anything else that could inhibit soldering; and, starting from the corner in the right-angle of your secured laths and lead, gradually build up your glass and lead, keeping the line of work progress as near as possible in a diagonal of 45°, across the bench.

The *tray* holding the glass to be glazed should be on the right-hand side; and the *tools* for glazing should be opposite you on the far side of the bench (but this side of the spare, stretched calmes).

The *tin of farriers' nails* to secure the glass could be on the left-hand side, beyond the base lath, because it is normal to feed them into position with the left hand—knocking them in with a hammer or a glazing knife held in the right hand.

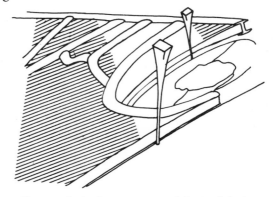

122 *Keeping the lead in position with farriers' nails*

Mark, in your mind's eye, or on the cutline, which width of lead you require, because the panel will need different leads and these must be anticipated. See, too, which are the main leads of the design, so that when there is a cross joint, i.e. one lead running through another, you will know which of them should carry through and take precedence over the other. If such a decision is not relevant to the design, it is always best to remember, as a general rule, that all *long* leads run to their height. In other words, always join across horizontal leads, leaving the vertical ones intact. This will give the panel greater strength, and help to prevent buckling in years to come.

Avoid having leads trailing from your work across the bench, as these will become damaged and bent, besides being difficult to work with, it will spoil the look of the lead; there is a limited number of times that lead calmes can be re-stretched.

Always see that the glass is firmly, and correctly, in place with nails, and that the lead follows the exact size and shape of the glass.

Make sure that the glass has fitted into the lip or leaf of the lead, particularly if it is a thick piece of glass. The thickness of the glass can be reduced by grinding it away on the unpainted side, or accommodated by pinching the heart of the lead with criss-cross pinches of the pincers; if this is done, the passage may have to be reinforced and strengthened over the criss-cross with a little solder—a tricky operation.

Make sure that the glass and lead are in position properly and fitted snugly together, and that one piece of glass is a similar shape to the edge adjoining it; also that there are no corners or bumps sticking out to prevent the two pieces of glass and the heart of the lead from fitting tightly together. The lead joints must be well made, and have no gaps. A good practice in joining leads is to lift the leaf of the existing lead slightly where you are going to abut another lead, and insert the second lead underneath. This makes a very much more solid joint.

When you cut the lead, make sure that the cut is straight down and at right angles unless it is going to meet the lead intentionally at an angle—in which case the angle *must* be judged correctly. It is amazing how many beginners get the *angle* correct but cut in the wrong position: in fact, handed. They then attempt to solder a joint that has exposed the heart of the lead to one of the pieces of glass and it ends up in a point. A little extra trouble cutting the lead at this stage saves endless trouble and patching when the soldering has to be done. If you have to join a rounded or other shape encompassed with one piece of lead, make the joint coincide with another joint. If this is not done, and a joint is soldered along a straight

passage of lead between glass, there is a grave risk of the glass cracking, owing to the heat; and an even greater likelihood of the glass breaking when pressure is applied whilst cementing, because often there is a drop of solder lodging under the joint of the lead, which presses into the surface of the glass on being cemented, and causes a crack or fracture (see diagram 124).

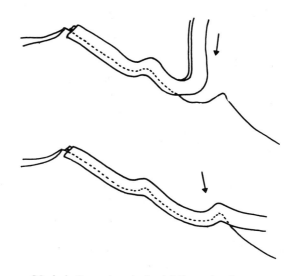

123 *Method of assuring the lead follows the glass*

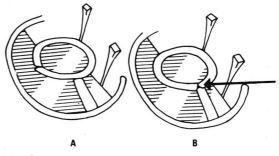

124 A *wrong way*
B *right way of joining circular lead to other calme*

It requires a great deal of experience to be able to bend the lead exactly to the shape of the glass, using the lathekin. When beginning glazing, it is best to work the lead actually on the glass in the hand, before putting both on to the glazing bench into their final position. Judging the exact position at which to cut off the lead, so that it is just the right length when fitted, always takes time, too; it is always worth exaggerating the lengths and then trimming off afterwards.

When you secure the glass, place a small piece of lead against the glass before knocking in a glazing nail. This length of lead should have two side leaves cut off to accommodate the nail; the other two leaves hold the piece of glass firm and prevent the shelling of the painted surface by the rough contact of the nail.

Cutting the lead is done in various ways—one way is to press down on the butt of the knife-handle vertically over the lead; another, for wide leads, is to use the side of the knife cutting-edge as a fulcrum, and to bear down on the lead. In the case of using a German curved lead knife, bearing down on the lead with a swinging action towards you is the only possibility. When using an English lead knife vertically on a lead which could be tough, it is always a good practice to oscillate the knife handle quickly several times up and down the length of the lead as you are cutting it (like the vibrato action of a violin-player), this tends to open up the fissure in the lead that the knife has begun to make, and makes for a good clean cut.

Steel-core lead is used generally when there is a large area of glass that needs strengthening, and where a tie or saddle-bar is artistically inappropriate. It can also be used for one of the main upright leads running through the panel.

Steel core is made either with the steel completely enveloped in the heart of the lead (see the lead diagram) or as a steel stiffening band, which is inserted by the glazier in an ordinary lead, together with the glass, in the course of glazing. This can be purchased either in lengths or in coil form. The lengths are the best to buy. Avoid the coil, because it is extremely difficult to undo and to make it remain flat. Generally speaking, made up steel cored lead calme is good enough in most cases but it needs an adjustment to the cutline. This is more considerable than the

adjustment needed in freely inserted steel core. With regard to the latter it can definitely be an advantage, especially where high heart lead is used for plating. If free steel is inserted in division leads it should obviously be on the *under* side of the *under* lead for protection from the weather.

'*Full*' and '*Slack*'

'*Full*' means that, owing to inaccurate cutting of the pieces of glass, and inattention in grozing them down to the right size during glazing, the panel works out to be too big in all directions. '*Slack*' is just the opposite. Owing to the glass being cut too small during cutting and being leaded-up without *packing* or using wider leads, the panel works out to be too small for the final perimeter marked on the cutline.

It is difficult to say which is the more annoying situation. 'Full' is easier to deal with than 'slack'. The *packing* of the leads, referred to above, is the insertion of small slips of lead into the space between the leaves of the lead before it is placed hard up against the piece of glass that is slack. The lead acts as a pad to take up the unwanted room left by the slack cutting of the glass.

When you have reached the edge of the panel you are glazing make absolutely sure it is straight and even. When the time comes to put the outer flat-lead on, make sure that the top leaf of the lead is opened evenly and widely first. This ensures that there is no possibility of the lead catching on the ends of the panel leads, and sending the whole panel awry. The lead and glass may have to be gently lifted a little with the glazing knife, so as to allow the lower leaf of the outer lead to slip neatly under the butt ends of the panel leads without disturbance. All these actions are done with the oyster or stopping-knife.

It is more normal to fit on the outer flat-lead edge prior to putting on the top-lead, which should be the last lead to go on the panel but sometimes the action is reversed and the top goes on before the side. For setting in stonework the top lead always stretches the full width of the panel, however. When both the outer leads are in position, fit a straight strip of 0·90 kg (32 oz) glass, 50 mm to 102 mm (2 in. to 4 in.) wide, along the *length* of the panel (tucked neatly into the outer leaves of the flat lead, and hard up against the heart all the way along) and across the *top*—then, with a small block of wood used as a kind of punch and a hammer, gently knock the panel tight to the correct size, always remembering not to distort it out of square.

When you have made quite certain that the panel is the correct size, fix the strips of glass securely on the outside to keep the panel quite firm and stable by banging glazing nails along the outer edge, then go over the whole surface of the panel, line up any of the leads that might have shifted out of shape slightly, straighten any that are twisted, lift the corners of the lead at the joints with the oyster-knife (they may have been depressed out of shape in the act of pressing down with the cutting-knife) so as to make a good flat joint, and check that the whole panel has not bulged upwards in the middle whilst being subjected to the pressure of being knocked up.

Now is the time to make good any small errors in the length of the lead calmes used, inserting little wedges of lead to help fill in and bridge the gaps. If the leads are uneven, i.e. at slightly different levels where they join it helps the act of soldering if you give them a tap at the junctures with a small hammer to flatten them completely. Also if any leads are wildly different in height, for instance at a point of transition between ordinary lead and wide-heart lead (used in plating), the lower lead can be gently flanged up to meet the higher, and the wide-heart lead can be fully hammered down at a slope to meet the lower lead. Any leads that are visibly old and dirty would benefit at this time by being cleaned with a scratch-card or an emery cloth.

Gently tap down all the joints where the inside lead meets the outer lead, making them even and true; and finally, free the surface of the panel of all little pieces of lead, glass, dust, and splinters. Brush all over the panel lightly with the scrubbing brush (not too hard, as this will twist the leads or push them out of shape); then take a stick, or half a stick, of soldering tallow flux, and liberally rub every joint with it.

During glazing, I usually have two tin lids and a badger brush by me. One tin lid holds the farriers' nails, and is on the left as I have described; the other lid is used to hold all the scraps of lead chippings and small lengths—keeping them out of the way, and clear of the work. I think a small pottery or wooden porringer could be an advantage over a tin lid because of the ease with which, in the case of nails, you can scoop them out. It pays to have a badger brush handy, to brush away any chippings of glass that accumulate on the bench during grozing, and which always have a habit of sticking to one's knuckles when one is in the middle of an intricate passage of glazing. If grozing is necessary, it should be done over the side of the bench onto the floor, when chippings will be swept up at the end of the day's work. If, as I suggested, a duckboard is used to stand on, the glass chips should not grate under foot. If the grozing *must* be done over the bench, do not do it over the work already done, but well away, and use the badger brush to keep the splinters of glass at bay.

Glazing plating

It is best to mark the cutline with a coloured chalk on areas that are plated, so that the glazier can anticipate these passages, and put in the appropriate double, or wide-heart, lead. Nothing is more annoying then to complete the leading of a passage and find that the next piece of glass is plated. The two pieces of glass making up the plated passage should be grozed, so that they are as near a perfect fit as possible; otherwise, in time, they tend to work loose by shifting and see-sawing against each other, in position, and this is what gives plating a bad name.

Another precaution that is sometimes taken with plating is to bind together both pieces of glass round the edges with Scotch tape before inserting them both into the leading. I find this theoretically a good idea, but really rather a waste of time. It is very much to the point, however, in glazing plating, to see that the two pieces of glass are good companions, and that one does not oscillate or rock up and down on the other, owing to their original shape, or subsequent distortion in the process of firing. For the same reason it is inadvisable to plate two pieces of Norman slab together, or a slab reversed with its bump side towards a piece of antique glass.

As in cutting, it is advisable to wear boots of some sort whilst working, rather than sandals or shoes, which can collect numerous little pieces of glass.

Glazier's pie

This term refers to the rising up of the middle of a panel of unsoldered glazing, owing to the pressure the glazier puts on the outer edge of the panel. Something has to give, and usually the whole of the middle of the panel lifts. This is more likely to occur when the panel contains many horizontal or vertical parallel leads, and pressure is being put on them sideways. More often than not, the occurrence of glazier's pie is very dramatic and sudden, and can ruin a day's work, as well as leading to the smashing of glass. If it looks likely that pie will occur, it is best to weight the panel down in the middle with lead weights—failing that, take out the leads in the last passages of your glazing and groze the glass that needs it carefully, to effect a truer fit—and release the sideways pressure that otherwise would build up. This may be tedious but in the long run it is better than ruining the whole panel through obstinacy.

Soldering

The soldering-iron is the instrument that transfers heat from the gas flame to the point you want to solder. Originally it was, in fact, made of iron, but now, though retaining the name, it is always made of copper—since this is a far more efficient conductor of heat.

Types of soldering-iron

1 *Electric* Though very efficient for electrical, radio and other purposes, the electrical soldering-iron is not so useful for stained glass, because it is not nearly as flexible in use as gas. The heat is generated in a small coil or heating used on a continuous job of soldering. They are expensive to buy. Electric soldering-irons, however, are used, I am told, in every American studio. In that case they must be vastly superior to English ones.

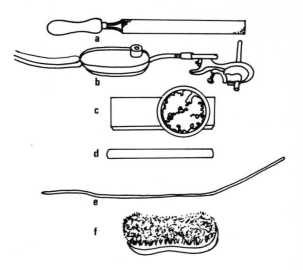

125 *Soldering equipment*
  a *file*   d *tallow stick*
  b *modified gas soldering-iron*   e *solder*
  c *tinning tin*   f *brush*

2 *Gas* The gas soldering-iron is satisfactory because it is quite controllable. It consists of a gas jet which is played through an air intake, like a bunsen burner on to a copper bit of 6 or 9 mm ($\frac{1}{4}$ or $\frac{3}{8}$ in.) copper, about 102 mm (4 in.) long. You usually have to make a shield yourself out of a small piece of metal strip bent in a circle and fit it as best you can to make sure the gas flame does not pass beyond the copper bit, but continues to play all round it. (See diagram) The copper bit sticks out at the top of the soldering-iron at the opposite end to the soldering surface, partly as an economy, i.e. a reservoir of copper that can gradually be tapped forward to make good the copper lost in trim and soldering and partly as a storage for heat. The copper is secured to the rest of the soldering-iron through a collar with a grub-screw, and can be advanced as the activity of soldering eats away the other end.

The jets in gas soldering-irons depend on the amount of pressure going through the gas system; also you must have the correct jet in the soldering-iron for the gas you are using, otherwise it will not work.

The air-control sleeve is a small angular flat

ring of metal very much like the air control on a bunsen burner; the ring should not be made as tight as that however: it should be loose enough to be able to be flicked to and fro by a quick action of the solder stick. Since no makers of soldering irons seem ever to have thought of it you usually have to make it by hand and fit it yourself. This creates the difference between the passive flame (no air intake) and the active flame (much air intake). The passive flame is allowed to play while the soldering-iron is not immediately being used; when you wish to heat up the iron, slide the air-control sleeve to let in as much air as possible. The flame at once changes character, becoming hotter, bluer, and fiercer. When you think that the flame has heated the soldering-iron enough, it is best to test it on a sample piece of lead kept to hand.

The soldering-iron Clean the soldering-iron in the following way. If it is badly pitted at the end, or if it is very dirty and untinned, file it smooth and even, first on a rough file, then on a *clean* fine one. Heat the soldering-iron to a dull red heat, i.e. the copper begins to blush purple and then coat the end with tin.

The tinning tin is made by nailing a tin lid with the depression uppermost on to a wooden handle, and filling the top of the lid with a *little* tallow and *more* powdered resin. The wooden handle permits the glazier to hold on to the tin whilst the soldering-iron is being rubbed hard on to the tin lid. Before rubbing hard with the soldering-iron, melt a generous amount of solder into the lid. The resin frequently ignites at this point, but it is easy to blow out, and does no harm. When the face of the soldering-iron is correctly and uniformly tinned, it has a very

pleasant ease of movement, and no longer feels gritty and awkward—a glissading feeling in fact—when moved backwards and forwards. If the soldering-iron refuses to tin and remains murky and patchy, the only thing to do is to wipe it quickly with a clean cloth laid on the bench, refile with the smoother file, and try again, using perhaps more solder. Frequently, unless the soldering-tin is swimming in solder, the iron finds it difficult to take to the solder.

When properly tinned, the end of the soldering-iron should look mirror-bright and smooth. Do not think that the tin has an unlimited life. Usually a few months and you have to chuck it away as being too congested with solder and carbonized fluxing agent to do its job properly.

Technique

Having tinned the soldering-iron and heated it to the right heat, cut off the air supply, and set the iron on a stand to your right. Have a supply of tallow and a supply of blowpipe solder to your left.

Blowpipe solder is a very thin solder, never more than 5 mm ($\frac{3}{16}$ in.) wide, which is ideal for leaded light glazing. Any other form of solder, either in bar form or circular in section with flux in the middle, is no use for stained glass work at all. Solder is expensive because it has a very high percentage of tin in it, and it is best to keep all the little ends of 50 mm (2 in.) or so and put them aside—when you have sufficient stubs to make sticks, simply melt them together one following the other and continue to use as if it were a new stick of solder.

Generously tallow the joints of the lead, and then check up that you have done them all—one always misses out one or two.

Start your soldering on the outside joints. Firmly hold the soldering-iron in one hand usually the right, and a stick of blowpipe solder in the other. Hold the copper straight and square on the joint until you can see the solder run to the edges of the joint, then lift the iron clear of the work. Only by practice and experience will you be able to gauge when the copper of the soldering-iron is at the right temperature.

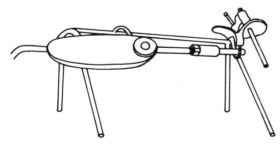

126 *Soldering iron on stand*

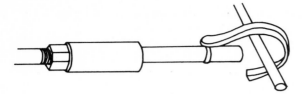

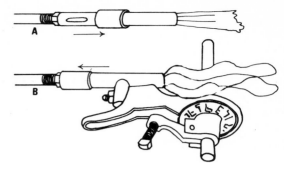

127 Showing bent tin guard to keep heart of flame on the copper (bracket holding copper omitted)

128 A active flame   B passive flame

Soldering that can go wrong

Faults 1 If the solder refuses to melt, even under pressure from the copper, or if, having melted, a little solder goes into a point like a small pyramid on the join when you pull the soldering-iron clear —the copper is too cool.

2 If the lead disintegrates under the slightest pressure of the copper the soldering-iron is too hot. A great hole gaping at you is the most unpleasant result. This can be avoided by testing on a piece of lead as I formerly suggested.

3 If the solder after melting seems incapable or reluctant to spread in a silver circle over the lead, and remains in gobbets after removing the soldering-iron, it means that the leads are dirty. They must be scraped with a scratch card or emery paper, re-tallowed, and tried again. The soldering-iron may have got dirty, too, and should be checked.

4 If the soldering goes off well and then for some unknown reason becomes less and less efficient however much you press and heat up the copper, it usually means that the copper itself is in need of a file-down and re-tin. With use it gets very pitted at the end because hot solder tends to act as a solvent on the copper bit and thus the transfer of heat becomes inefficient.

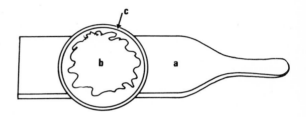

129 Tinning tin
    a wood
    b solder
    c tin

130 Solder too hot

Sequence of soldering

Having soldered all the outside joints it is quite safe to take out the knocking-up wood or glass strips together with their retaining nails. Solder all the joints systematically, working your way across the panel from bottom to top (if you are right-handed). Never advance the hand holding the iron over the places you have soldered when they could be hot.

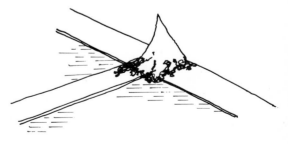

131 Solder too cool

Be careful when reaching across the panel because, as well as the risk of burning yourself, you may well break the glass by leaning too hard on it or by touching it accidently with the hot soldering-iron.

If the soldering-iron is at the right temperature and the leads are clean and level, and well tallowed, the art of soldering should become a pleasure, but this does depend very much on careful preparation.

Once you have finished your soldering, put the iron clear of the work, on the stand provided, turn the gas low and then scrub off the surplus flux or tallow with the scrubbing brush so as to leave it quite clean and shining. It is now, after scrubbing, that it is as well to go over the panel with your eye to see if you have missed a joint or two—they are very easily distinguished at this stage.

Remove the nails securing the panel round the outside if you have not already done so, also the lath of wood or strip of glass, and ease the panel away from the two fixed laths keeping it flat on the bench.

Rub down the outer leaves of the outer leads at an angle of about 30°.

Turning over the panel

When the first side of the panel has been soldered, the other side has to be done. Turning the panel over, if it is a small one, is quite easily done, but if it is any width or size at all this action can be quite tricky. The panel is only soldered one side and is extremely flimsy, and stands a good chance of buckling.

Method

Either lift the panel's front edge over the fixed lath running along the front of the bench, or better still push the panel over the other side of the bench, if you can, where there is no lath; then pull the panel half off the bench, still keeping it horizontal, not lifting it off the bench at all, and with one hand supporting the front edge and the other hand prepared to support the weight of the rear edge, tilt the whole panel over towards you, taking the weight with both hands, but also keeping the centre of the panel supported by the edge of the bench which acts as a fulcrum or turning point of balance. When the panel is vertical it is perfectly safe; you can lift it up on to the bench and stand it upright. Next move the panel as far back as you can reach, or as far back as is necessary to lie it flat in front of you. Remove your hands from the top edge and place them both in the middle of the panel, supporting it with your fingers outstretched. Then gently lower towards you until the panel is resting on your forearms and the palms of your hands. Lower gently all the time, at the same time slowly pulling your hands out from underneath. The movement from the vertical to the horizontal is in fact a very swift movement, half taking advantage of the pull of gravity. It is more of a controlled fall, pivoting on the edge of the panel which lies along the bench.

When the panel is flat, check that the edges of the outer lead are not bent backwards. Straighten them out by means of the stopping knife. Check again that all your glass is in the lead. You will now be able to see if you have cut your leads straight whilst glazing. If you have not cut the leads straight you will find that big holes previously invisible on the other side of the panel have been left. These holes should be patched with small wedges and slivers of lead. All glass that is standing proud of the lead calme must be carefully coaxed under the leaf, and the lead calme straightened into its rightful position. Joints should be gone over in exactly the same way as on the previous side, all the corners being lifted or tapped. You must not forget to clean off the whole panel with the scrubbing brush when you have finally finished soldering. Clean up the joints to be soldered with scratch card or emery paper, rub the joints with the tallow stick, and begin to solder on this side. When the panel is soldered on both sides, even though it may not yet be cemented, it is quite rigid and secure and can be handled with safety in an upright position. The finished panel is then stored in the racks running under the glazing bench, and is ready for cementing.

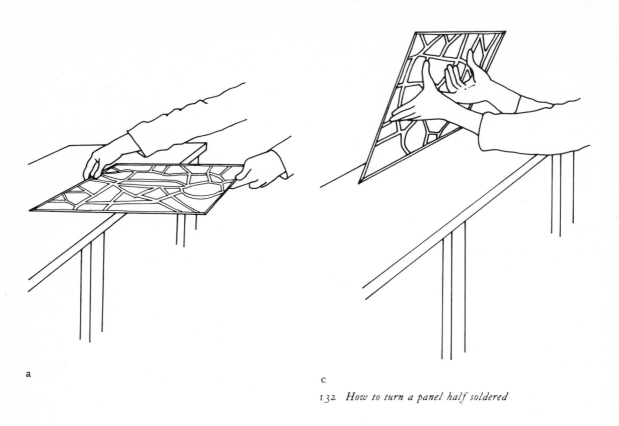

a

c

132 *How to turn a panel half soldered*

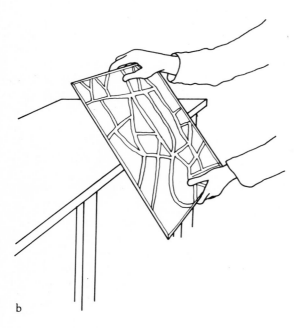

b

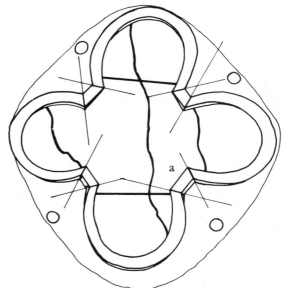

133 *Showing angles to be cut in lead quatrefoil glazing*

Specialised glazing techniques

Glazing of traceries Remember, with traceries it is always best to make them too small, as the fixers can make up the deficiency, if it occurs, with mortar; but if the tracery light is too big, either the cusping and the tracery have to be abused to get it in, or the stained glass ends up back on your door-step and has to be modified at your expense. Also you receive an additional bill from the fixers for the time and work and extra hiring of scaffolding.

Cut and shape all the outside leads before starting to glaze, calculating all the correct angles where they fit together by comparing them with those lines you have drawn. Fit all the outer leads together on the cutline first, so that they will finish correctly when glazed.

Glazing of traceries

1 *Straight-sided traceries* These may be glazed in the ordinary way, beginning from one or the other of the straight sides and building up towards the most complicated cusped points top and bottom.

2 *Irregular traceries* These can be glazed from the outside across to the opposite side, but I have always found the best way is to start in the middle and work outwards all round, keeping the pressure of the work equal by means of very many firmly tapped farriers' nails.

Apart from the initial border lead on the straight outer side, the edge leads are invariably the last ones to be fitted on traceries. The cutline of the tracery (and that of the head of the window too, if it is cusped) should be marked with a pencil line parallel to the already marked border-line 6 mm ($\frac{1}{4}$ in.) away all the way round on the outside. At the intersection of the cusping (see diagram) an axial line should be drawn exactly bisecting the angle the cusps make where they join. This will indicate the angle at which to cut the edge-lead so as to effect a perfect balanced and even meeting. If the cusps have chamfered points, which they often do have, blunted, triangular or a number of cuts in the edge lead around the cusp-line will have to be made depending on the number of angles in the turn of the cusp. On no account

torture the edge-lead back upon itself to twist round the cusping and up to the next bulge. This always looks unsightly, usually works out very inaccurate, and may end in disaster.*

The glass round the edges of the cusping and tracery in general should always be grozed away to leave it about 6 mm ($\frac{1}{4}$ in.) short of the first marked edge-line. The lead, well widened with the lathekin and shaped to the correct shape beforehand, should be so placed as to come inside the second outer, recently marked, edge-line. In this way the tracery lights will fit into the tracery of the window with no trouble at all. Do not forget that to glaze the perimeter of a tracery light curve you will always need a longer outer lead calme than you anticipate.

All soldering around the edge-leads, in the cuts round the cusping for instance, must be done only towards the interior of the glass using very little solder (on both sides) half across, not right across, the edge-lead. The reason for this is that if you solder right across the lead, the hardness of the solder prevents the fixer from bending the lead efficiently to get it in the groove.

Division-leads

Owing to the division of the glass into panels, an efficient and water-tight method of leading where two panels join is essential. When the light is being glazed and, at the end of the panel, you reach the division, put a narrow, flat lead across the top of the panel, having made certain that the glass is extremely carefully and evenly lined up

---

* When glazing the tracery and fashioning the outside lead to fit the cutline in passages other than very tight cusps, if you do not use a lathekin and try to bend the lead with your hands, you will undoubtedly find that the lead will bend to a certain degree, then suddenly go at a sharp angle, causing the leaf to buckle on the inside of the bend, and possibly split on the outside. But if you hold one end of the lead with one hand, letting the other rest against the lath on the bench or on the inside of your forearm; then holding the lathekin in the other hand (using the curved or less pointed end of the lathekin) run it down the inside, against the heart of the lead several times, exerting a little more pressure each time, you will find that it will stretch the outside leaf, and the lead calme will bend smoothly.

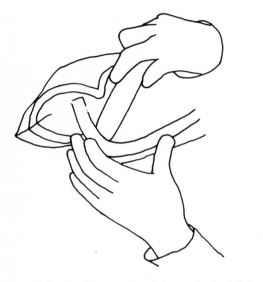

134 *How to shape tracery perimeter lead with lathekin*

along a line about 6 mm ($\frac{1}{4}$ in.) in from the top division line marked on the cutline. The top lead should be a flat-leaved lead, not a round-leaved one. When this is soldered into position, take care not to let the solder go right across the width of the top lead. Then rub down the outer leaves of the lead, the underneath one overlapping the top one so as to effectively diminish its width by almost one half.

Start the next section of the light by fitting a division-lead as it is called, over the top of the previous panel. Division-leads can be any width but are usually 12 to 15 mm ($\frac{1}{2}$ in. to $\frac{5}{8}$ in.) wide and are always flat-sectioned leads, never round. They can sometimes have an eccentrically placed heart, in which case the narrower half of the leaf

goes towards the edge of the glass and the wider towards the lap.

The larger lead on the bottom edge of the panel above, fitting into the smaller lead of the panel below, when both are fixed into position and puttied between, give a completely watertight joint to the window.

N.B. The fitting of the division-lead with the edge-lead in glazing the second panel; the joint is an abutment of the edge to the division-lead, not a mitre joint.

T-bar glazing
Sometimes, in a long light, the weight of the window is supported halfway down by a T-sectioned metal bar. When this occurs the panels top and bottom of the T-bar are ended (and begun) with 12 mm ($\frac{1}{2}$ in.) section flat lead. The joints at the corners may be mitred. The whole panel is then bedded against the cross of the T with the stem of the T bar (which projects horizontally) as a horizontal barrier between it and the panel immediately above.

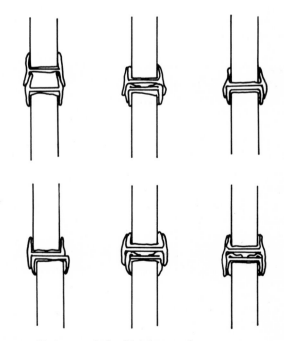

135 *Various methods of joining panels*

French glazing

Most French glass is still inserted in iron T-bar shapes; sometimes in random patterns, sometimes in rectangles. The individual panels are glazed with the appropriate flat lead all the way round and then inserted into the iron framework, embedded in putty or mastic. To keep the panels from falling inwards into the building (the T-bar being usually placed in the window with the stem of the T pointing towards the inside) the panels are wedged in by small metal wedges, stuck in through the stem of the T and projecting top and bottom, thereby stopping the glass from coming loose. In many cases in France the T-bar is fretted in such a way as to allow the superimposition of a template, which itself is secured by wedge-shaped pieces of metal, thereby completely enclosing the panel in a U-shaped seating of metal. Although the description of this method (which is, in effect the same as the original twelfth century method) seems heavy, the result, as you can see in the diagram is strong, stylish and elegant; but I think it is only appropriate in old French gothic buildings whether the glass is new, restored or ancient. It simply does not seem to fit the modern scene.

Owing to the thinness of the lead used in France, the individual panels are always too big and flimsy, so additional saddle-bars are braced across the panels but are not embedded or anchored into anything at either end. They simply float across the window at random and convenient angles and intervals, and are attached to the inner surface of the glass by means of whorls of lead which are about 32 mm ($1\frac{1}{4}$ in.) across when they have been completed. There is no doubt that, given the circumstances above, the French way of finishing glass in iron T-bars is far better and well worth the extra trouble and cost on a large job.

Solder

The actual solder joint takes some three seconds to harden. Before it is hardened, even though it may look solid, it can easily be torn apart since the solder is very brittle. The line of solidification and hardness can be seen travelling from each side of the soldered joint to meet in a slight demarcation in the middle. It is not safe to jerk or disturb the lead until the joining process has been seen to happen.

Sub-soldering

If certain passages are very difficult to glaze they may be pre-glazed and incorporated in the work as the glazing progresses. Do not underestimate the importance of working the glass and the lead together in the hand as well as on the bench. Similarly, if a passage which is being glazed shows signs of being troublesome in the future unless it is fixed in position in some way, it is perfectly all right to solder what has been done so far, providing it is not slack or full, and continue glazing in the normal way.

136 *Detail of leaded glass by Georg Meistermann showing virtuosity in leading*

137 *Magritte. Panel by Paul Marioni, 1975, showing
the possibilities of sandblasting*

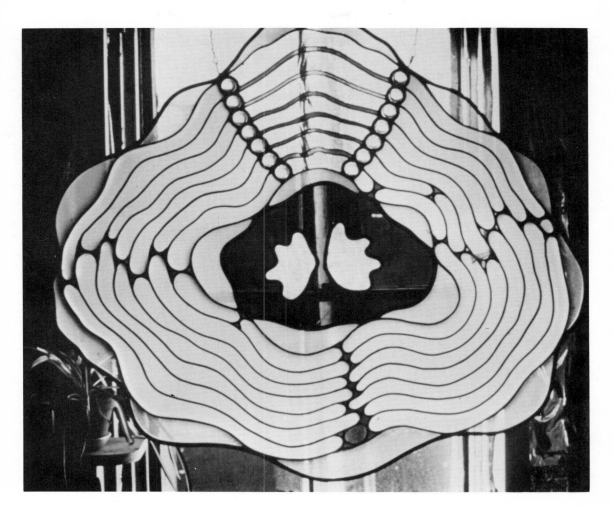

138 *Composition by Ray King. Philadelphia* 1977

139 *Detail of windows in the church of Notre-Dame*
Issy-les-Moulineux, Paris, designed by Léon Zack
1955, showing interesting contrasts in leading

140 *Church window composition by Georg Meistermann,*
executed by Hans B. Gossel, showing mastery
of leading

141 *Window designed by Ludwig Schaffrath at
St Michael, Schweinfurt, Germany*

Cementing

It is one of the indications of the relative way the cement is mixed in England and France that the term for the process in England is cementing whereas the French term is *graissage*. Cementing is essential to stained glass. It not only prevents the glass from rattling about in the leads, and keeps it waterproof, but it also makes the whole panel rigid and strong. There is the added reason that the action of cementing makes the *lead* sink into second place, bringing out the positiveness of the artistic statement in the *glass*. No one can properly criticise a stained glass panel that has not been cemented.

Pre-cementing technique

1 Make quite sure all the joints are soldered.
2 Check up as to whether there is any plating in the window. (If you have been methodical and put a wax pencilled P on the plated pieces immediately after scrubbing off the tallow, this should not be difficult.)

If there is plating, the following drill must be done. Mix the putty with sufficient black colouring matter to change its colour and enough boiled linseed oil to make it really plastic.

Lift the leads round the plating carefully with the glazing knife. With the thumb, push the putty well into the space between the leaf and the plating. Pressure must be brought to bear to force the putty well in; then, when the putty is in, press the lead leaf down again tightly against the plating, sealing quite a quantity of black putty inside. The remains of putty can be cleaned away with a knife and gathered together for further use by being mopped up with a ball of putty in the other hand.

Further puttying must be done round the exterior joints of the plating, but need not be continued along the straight side of the calme. The reason for these precautions is that if the cement, being far more runny than the putty, were allowed to flow freely round the unprotected plating it would seep into the space between the two pieces of glass, imprisoned as they are together in the lead, and produce what is known as 'a mushroom', i.e. a large semicircular stain of wet cement lodged between the two pieces of plating and incapable of being cleaned out and removed without an extensive emergency operation on the glazing which has just been completed.

In puttying, especially the special puttying for securing the waterproofness of plating, do not forget to turn the panel over and do exactly the same thing on the other side.

If the puttying is done an hour or so before the cementing it is advisable to remove the boiled linseed oil smudges on the glass on both sides with a turpentined cloth. They may be difficult to get off otherwise and will catch any dirt arising as a result of final polishing and finishing (i.e. with vegetable black, etc.).

Finally, before beginning to cement, gently open up the leads round the edges with the glazing knife so they may receive the cement.

Cement

Cement, which is distinguished from the ordinary cement used in building, is a loose mixture of boiled linseed oil, whitening, and some turps substitute. Some powdered red lead is added as a drying agent, and sometimes gold size, and the cement is usually coloured with vegetable black so that when it is in the lead it is not noticeable.

It can be bought ready made, but some think it better to make their own, as and when required.

Method

Using a small stick put a little cement in dollops all over the panel of glass which has been laid flat on the cementing table. It is not necessary to flood the panel with cement: a small amount is sufficient.

Then using a small but very firm scrubbing brush spread the cement evenly over the surface of the panel.

Next, with a sweeping wrist movement with a lift at the end (the tip of the brush rising over the lead, leaving a roll of cement under the leaf, which acts as a kind of scraper) make quite sure that the cement is under the lead leaf and all round the glass, i.e. between the section of the glass and the heart of the lead.

Continue this action on one side and turn over

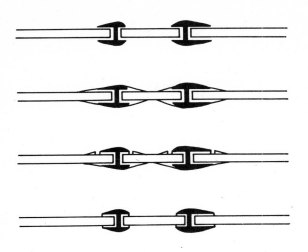

142 *Stages in section cementing*
    1 *raw leads*
    2 *lead with cement*
    3 *lead with cement half cleaned off*
    4 *fully picked off and polished*

the panel and repeat it thoroughly on the other side.

Every lead must be filled with cement—special care must be taken not to forget the corners. If leads look as if they are being forced down and not receiving the cement, flange them up with a sideways-running movement of the glazing knife to allow the free flow of the cement.

When the cement has been well scrubbed in, rub down the flat leads all round the edge of the panel till they are flat on the glass, and scrub off the surplus cement from the surface of the glass, scraping the scrubber on the side of the bucket to get rid of any excess cement. The glass and the leads should now be almost clean. Sprinkle the panel with a generous amount of powdered whitening and rub the panel all over with a cloth so that the whitening builds up on the edge of the lead, sticking to, and masking, the wet cement. Turn the panel over and do exactly the same on the other side, then stand the panel upright against a wall to dry.

Depending on the amount of dryer put into the mixture, and the weather, this can take as short a time as an hour and a half, or it may have to be left overnight.

When the cement is dryish (not rock hard) put the panel back on the bench, which has been swept clean of surplus cement and whitening and go round the inside perimeter of each piece of glass with a wooden stick which has been sharply pointed. The stick should be of wood because metal might scratch the glass. A good way of sharpening the stick is to make use of a small electric grindstone. At the same time you could smooth off the handle part of the pick, so that it fits with comfort in the palm of the hand.

Another pick to have handy is a chisel-shaped one. All the picks you use should be of the hardest wood you can get, such as beech, oak, holly or box. Occasionally for very small pieces of glass between leads a metal pick is useful. This could be made of a suitably filed down nail mounted in a wooden handle, but it should *not* be used as a matter of course. Scrape away all the surplus whitening and then brush the panel with a stiff brush to clean the glass and the leads thoroughly. I would emphasise that the cementing brush and the *cleaning brush* and the subsequent polishing brush, are three different brushes. Usually a brush starts by being a polishing brush, goes towards a cleaning brush, and ends up as a cementing brush.

The cementing table should be swept clean of powdered whitening between the sides of each panel to be cemented, to avoid the accidental packing of whitening under an unfilled lead. The result of such a packing is that sooner or later the window springs a leak. Only those who have had to waterproof a window on site, using ladders, know the agony and uncertainty of this performance.

When the leads are completely clean and polished, the panels are usually transported back to the glazing bench for a final inspection and a brisk polish with vegetable black or blacklead to smarten up the leads. At this stage look out for films of cement or oil on the painting on the inside of the glass. Sometimes, owing to the final firing of the glass not being hard enough, the matt texture of the paint tends to pick up the cement. If this is not rubbed off at the polishing stage with a turpentined rag the chances are that the true balance of paintwork on the glass may be darkened and upset for good, and much delicacy lost.

Cementing

During cementing it is possible (but not necessary) to get very dirty. As a help towards keeping clean, a very large simple smock worn over the clothes is a help. The sleeves should be a very close fit at the wrists. Rubber or leather gloves *can* be worn, but in general are a nuisance. Girls should cover their hair so as to avoid, during cementing, having to push it aside with heavy, cement-contaminated hand. The best way to remove cement from the hands is to rub them in olive oil and then wash them with soap and water. Detergents and scouring powders should not be used because of the real risk of dermatitis.

After cementing, the buckets and utensils must be cleaned thoroughly, otherwise what is left will go rock hard and ruin the insides of all the mixing buckets. A large amount of cement can be mixed and this will keep considerably longer if it is kept all together in a bucket with a layer of water on top. Before using the cement make sure all the water is removed.

Banding (wiring)

This process comes last of all in making stained glass windows. Bands may be made of lead, copper, or zinc and are fixed to the inside or outside of the window, to be wrapped round the saddle-bars going across the window and twisted round themselves on the outside of the bar, thus hugging the bar and the stained glass to each other.

The placing of the division- and the saddle-bars on the inside or the outside of the windows is really an aesthetic matter for the architect to decide. If the bars are on the outside they must be made of a reasonably non-corroding metal such as bronze, copper, or aluminium.

Saddle-bars

Saddle-bars are the generic name for all bracing bars, but there is a distinction made between those that go across the middle and those that are placed opposite the joint connecting two panels placed on top of one another, which are called division-bars. They are the same shape, section, and length, except that saddle-bars can be bent to different shapes to accommodate features in the window that should not be cut across.

Saddle-bars can be any section—square, round, or triangular. Round ones give a better seating to the copper or zinc ties on the glass, but square ones look infinitely better and are stronger.

Where saddle-bars occur across the window, the *ties* are soldered on to the leads, horizontally, along the line of the saddle-bar, never more than one every 63 to 76 mm ($2\frac{1}{2}$ to 3 in.). Ties are small lengths of copper wire (usually about 102 to 114 mm (4 to $4\frac{1}{2}$ in.) long) which are wrapped round the saddle-bar, turned round themselves, and cut off neatly. The twist is bent down, across, or along the saddle-bar.

Placing

The copper ties, as they are called, are sited where there is a joint already soldered in the course of glazing, and joints should be provided for the placing of the copper ties.

Method of making copper ties

1 Choose a good sectioned copper wire 16 to 18 gauge. After folding the end, put it either in a vice or round a convenient nail at the other end of the studio. Play out a long length of wire, say 4·5 m (15 ft) long, and let it lie on the ground, then with a piece of emery cloth folded round the wire, work backwards from the anchorage scouring the sides of the copper. to get it clean. When all 4·5 m (15 ft) have been done, fold the other end of the copper wire and stretch it vigorously. The straight clean wire can now be cut by gauge on the glazing bench into lengths of 102 mm (4 in.) or so. Lay these clean lengths in a line, parallel to one another, with about 12 mm ($\frac{1}{2}$ in.) gap between, along the length of either a piece of metal, glass or wood about 63 mm wide, 6 mm thick ($2\frac{1}{2}$ in. wide, $\frac{1}{4}$ in. thick), and 45 cm (18 in.) long, which has had a very generous piling of powdered fluxing resin spread along it. Nestle the copper wire pieces in the resin. Light the soldering-iron and put a small spot of solder on the centre of each

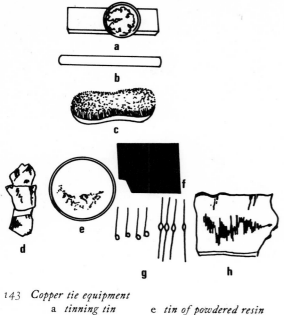

143 *Copper tie equipment*
- a *tinning tin*
- b *tallow stick*
- c *brush*
- d *block resin*
- e *tin of powdered resin*
- f *emery paper or cloth*
- g *copper ties*
- h *resin block*

round saddle-bars. Instead of soldering the wire at its centre and using both ends, only one end is used, the other being soldered to the top division-lead of one panel and it is matched by a reciprocal paired copper tie in the same position on the bottom division-lead of the panel above.

Method of making division copper ties
Division ties are essentially the same as ordinary copper ties, except that after cleaning, stretching, and gauge cutting the copper wire, one end of each piece of wire is bent over on to itself by about 6 mm ($\frac{1}{4}$ in.) turning it, in effect, into an object rather like a miniature golf stick. It is essential to bend the copper so that the end does *not* form a kind of round loop. The ties are laid down in the bed of powdered resin like the copper ties, but it is their

piece of copper, gently rolling it under the soldering-iron to make certain that the solder is attached all round the copper wire, not only on one side. The small cocoon-shaped piece of solder should look comfortable around the copper wire, having been moulded into shape by the action of the liquefied resin round it. Continue all the way along the line, and when the resin is firm again and the copper ties are *cool*, detach them and keep them. The whole resin line may go up in flames, but it is easy enough to blow out. Keep plenty of resin on the slab between making copper ties: the slab ought never to be allowed to go 'dry'.

These copper ties are very easy to attach to the places where needed, provided that these places have been scraped clean and tallowed. When you have finished soldering on the ties scrub the flux surrounding the seating of the copper ties off the surface of the panels.

Division-bars are the same shape and size as saddle-bars. The copper ties used round them differ considerably, however, from those used

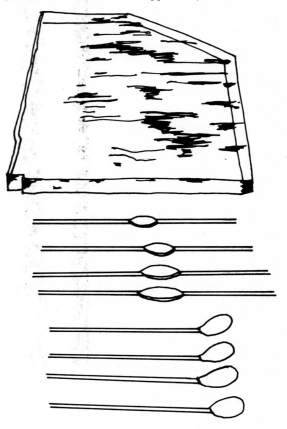

144 *A resin block and two kinds of copper tie*

heads that are coated with a blob of solder not their middles. Remove them when cold and attach as required to the stained glass panel which has previously been cleaned and tallowed. Remember the shaft of the division copper tie should lie over the opposite panel. Do not point the shaft of the tie into its own panel whilst soldering.

Attachment

Hold the stick at the end, with the head of solder on the proper place and press down with the hot soldering-iron. Scrub off tallow and melted bubbling cement.

Placing

Never stagger division ties, always pair them. In division ties it is important not to place the soldered heads right on the middle of the division lead, but more away to the centres of the panel, rather on the soldered lead calme as it meets the division-lead. This enables the leaf of the division lead of the panel above to ride over the top lead of the panel below without getting fouled on the seating of the copper ties. When the copper ties have been soldered on to the division-leads top and bottom, they should look in the same relationship to one another as one's interlaced straight fingers do. Pull the panels horizontally apart, and bend the copper ties along the length of the division lead or backwards, flush with the panel, so that they are conveniently out of the way until they are wanted.

Spare copper ties, if they have not all been used, should be carefully wrapped in greaseproof paper and kept for another time.

If there are any pinholes these should be· filled in with putty. If there are any cracks, a strap-lead may be put across the crack. A strap-lead

145 *Glazing resin—used as flux*
    a *lump resin*
    b *crushed resin on glass slab*

is usually made by slicing the leaf off a round-sectioned lead of the judged width, and having cut it to the right length, placing it along the crack, abutting to the lead calme on either side, or tucking it slightly in under the leaf, and soldering either end to the glazing already done. In any case you will have to clean up with a scratch cloth or emery paper the place where the strap lead meets the calme, and also remember that some cement may have to be scraped out to ensure a good solder joint. Then putty all round and clean. Finally place a small sectional lead in between the leaves of the wide division-lead and fix it in position by rubbing down either side with the glazing knife or lathekin. When the window is installed the small lead can be stripped out easily, leaving the division calme undamaged and ready to receive the top lead of the panel immediately under it.

Polish and store the glass ready for packing.

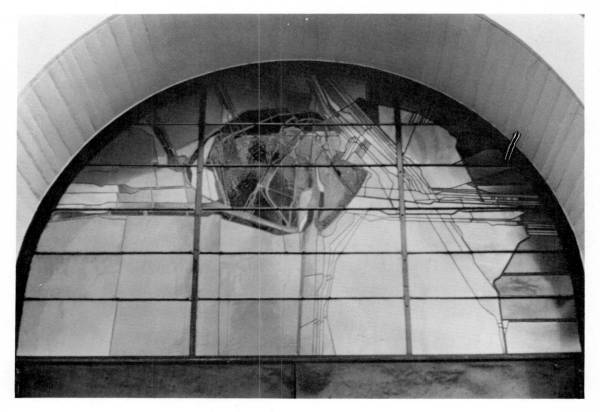

146 *Exterior window, Aldenhove, designed by Ludwig Schaffrath*

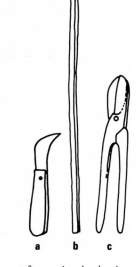

147 *Equipment for casting lead calmes*
   a *knife*
   b *cast*
   c *shear (clipper)*

148 *Lead melting bucket*

Every studio in France and Germany casts and extrudes its own lead calmes for use as required. Certainly home-drawn lead is extremely pleasant to work with, though rather a performance to make. A home lead-milling unit adds immeasurably to the quality of the finished work. It is almost a necessity for great achievement in stained glass.

Melting the lead
Lead is best bought from a reputable scrap merchant, in piglead ingots, and of course all the scraps of lead in the studio can be used up at the same time.

Buy a cast-iron crucible from the ironmonger, in which to melt the lead. It is best to build the crucible into a small brick bay with the bottom suspended over a calor- or coal-gas ring. The brick bay prevents any heat being wasted. Have the room well ventilated—the smell of lead melting, added to the smell of gas, is most unpleasant. Put sufficient lead into the crucible, and as it is heating up and melting put the iron moulds across the top so as to pre-heat them. This will make the casting of the lead far easier when the time comes.

When the lead is fully molten, skim off the dross (a kind of sulphur-like layer), and throw it away. Then carefully take the moulds off the top and secure them firmly to a wall or the side of a table or bench at about hip height. Open up the moulds and polish them on the inside with black lead or grate black. Close them again and with a full ladle pour the lead into the top of the mould, at the same time firmly press down the handle of the mould so that the two halves make a really good close fit together. Watch the lead rise to the top of the mould, and then stop pouring and wait until it settles. The handle of the lead ladle will get very hot and should be wrapped round with a cloth.

When the lead has settled, open up the mould, grasp the top of the cast with a pair of pincers, and with a sharp pull from top to bottom you should be able to get the cast out. Several attempts may be necessary before you get a complete casting.

When the castings can be handled, *hold the bottom* of them and dip the solid head of lead into the molten lead in the crucible. This separates the casts (in the case of multiple casting) and returns the blob of lead to the pot where it can be re-used in casting.

The casts are now ready for milling. The thickness of the milling can be varied with the different-sized cheeks which are supplied to slip into the lead mill. Before pushing the casting into the mill it is advisable to wipe them with a lightly oiled rag. This will give a better quality to the lead calme as it is milled.

Always carry out the instructions sent with the lead mill and keep it greased and oiled, and covered up or put away when not in use.

Always anticipate what lead you require and mill the *correct* casting in the correct cheeks when you want it. Castings can be kept many months without deterioration and can be milled into calme whenever wanted.

Always wear boots for casting lead. A shoeful of molten lead causes irritation.

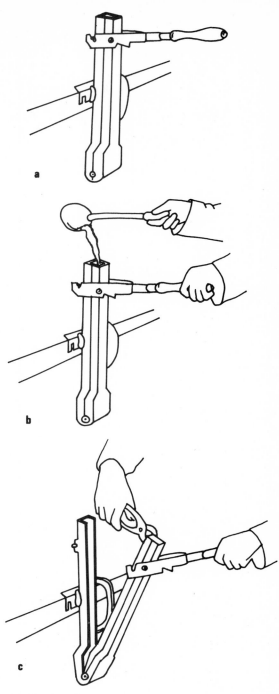

149 *Ladle and cloth handle*

150 *Lead casting*
    a *the mould*
    b *casting the lead*
    c *extracting the cast*

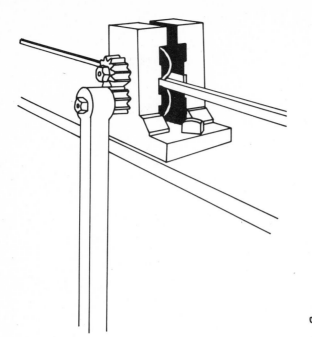

151 *Lead mill*

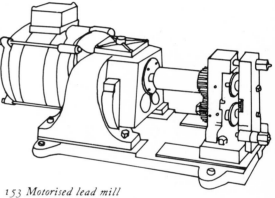

153 *Motorised lead mill*

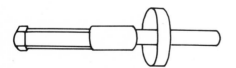

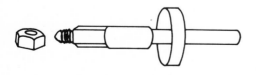

152 *Two spindles and cheeks for the lead mill*

Packing

When packing up glass to be sent by road or rail, bear two things in mind that:

1 porters are not by nature gentle people;
2 there is not often a forklift truck to help move crates in transport depots.

Therefore do not make the crate too heavy; two people should be able to lift it.

A crate for leaded lights should be no wider than 30 to 50 cm (18 to 20 in.).

Pre-packing note Number the stained glass panels by sticking on labels with adhesive tape and make sure that the numbers correspond to the numbers on the fixing diagram.

Materials

Straw This is not used much; it is not easy to get these days, and, as there are import/export embargoes on straw, it is best avoided.

Wood wool is efficient and good, at a reasonable price. It can be employed over and over again. But when it comes in a 100 kg (2 cwt) bale, it is very tightly compressed, and needs teasing out by hand before using. Wood wool should never be used in the tightly compressed state.

Expanded polystyrene is expensive and difficult to pack tight enough round the glass, but is useful for packing when there is a lot of space to fill up. It fills up space without adding to the weight.

Foam rubber chips Together with polystyrene, this is the best packing for anything that has a raised passage, or protuberance, but it is not as solid a packing material as wood wool, and objects packed in foam rubber have been known to move about within the packing case.

Method

Stand the crate in a position where it will not tilt over. Line the base of the box with a thick, even layer of wood wool. Sort out the panels into sizes, if they differ at all. Stand the largest in the centre, diminishing to the smallest on either outer side. Between each panel of glass there should be a sheet of corrugated paper or corrugated cardboard, or, failing that, at least two sheets of newspaper. This acts as a cushion between one panel and another by taking up all uneveness in the surfaces of the panels. Obviously if there is Norman slab in the window, extra packing between the glass should be used. Avoid any overlapping and irregularity in the placing of the panels in the box as this will probably endanger the glass. The panels (when packed together) should have a 50 or 76 mm (2 or 3 in.) space for wood wool all round.

As you pack, have someone to hold all the panels upright, while you push the wood wool evenly and very firmly round the glass. Do not try to pack one side at a time. Make quite sure when the panels are put in, that the bottom edge of each is close up to its neighbour, not half an inch away. Pay special attention to the ends of the crate, which should be tightly packed with wood wool otherwise the glass panels in the middle will move *en bloc* from end to end of the crate. Wooden rams to pack the wood wool down are useful when there is not room enough to slip your hand and forearm between the glass and the crate.

The great principle in packing is not to exert

any lateral pressure or tension on the glass as it is packed in the crate.

Final packing drill

When the wood wool has been packed level with the top of the glass, do not forget to put into the crate a *description of the contents,* so that whoever unpacks it, if they are not familiar with the window, can sort it out easily. This especially applies when there are several crates belonging to the same window or a series of windows. The situation demands it even more if they are windows with tracery because it is very easy to mislay small pieces.

Pack into the top of the crate a *fixing plan* as seen from either outside or inside (but be quite

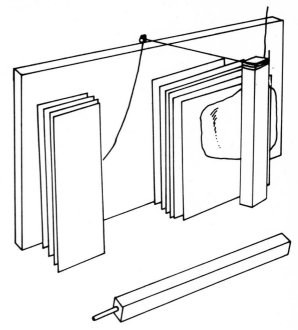

155 *Method of packing leaded glass for transport*

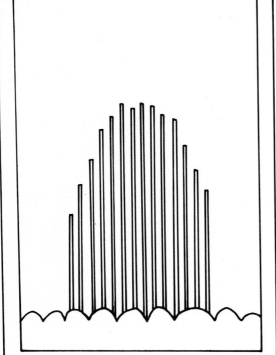

154 *Showing method of stacking glass panels in crate before packing*

specific which) and this must be checked to be in exact correspondence with the numbering of the panels just packed. An identical copy of this must be sent to the fixers and the clients or architects. Pack the top of the crate as full as possible with wood wool and nail or screw down. Finally, have the cases stencilled with your name and address if you want them returned, and have a prominent notice made with '*DO NOT LAY FLAT*' written on it, on two or three faces of the crate, because most transport people will certainly lay the crate flat and use it as a basis on which to pile other goods.

Just before nailing down it is as well to check who is responsible for *saddle-bars* and include them if it is yourself.

Delivery of glass to site
By far the most satisfactory method is to use your own transport and deliver to the site yourself. A small van is best for this. *Private cars*, apart from a shooting brake, are not good because you cannot prevent the glass moving about while driving. With a *van* the best way of packing the glass is edgeways to the motion of the vehicle. Place polystyrene, strawboard, or wood wool on the floor of the van where the glass is going to be placed. The best support for glass is a light frame constructed to lie back at a slight angle from the vertical. This 'fraille' as it is known, can be stored, and securely fixed in the van temporarily when you need it. Stack the glass in order, leaning on the fraille and keep it in position by a pole made of 50 mm × 50 mm (2 in. × 2in.) wood with a length of metal about 50 mm (2 in.) long inserted in the bottom of it. The metal prong should engage in a hole drilled in the floor at the base of the stack of glass panels. A shock-absorbing wad should be inserted between the pole and the face of the glass, and the top of the pole tied securely to the top of the fraille with a stout cord.

Fixing

Even today the fixing procedure has not altered much since medieval days, except that the tools and equipment are better.

Old fixing-mortar was a mixture of stone dust, sand, and lime and it still has its uses in certain circumstances. The new mastics used for fixing have, however, largely superseded mortar. Care should be taken when choosing a fixing mastic to avoid one that stains the surrounding stonework with oil.

The rebates, or the grooves, have to be thoroughly cleaned out before the window is installed. This is particularly important in the case of an old building. Stonework should be checked for crumbling at the same time.

In the case of *grooves* notice that one upright side groove is usually far deeper than the other.

Method

When all the grooves have been cleaned, place the bottom section of stained glass in position, by pushing it first into the deeper groove. Then straighten the panel up and ease it back into the groove on the other side, until the centre of the outside leads are on a line with the side-plane of the mullion.

Mark where the bar is going. Take out the panel of glass and make the hole for the bar, deeper on one side than on the other. Replace the panel and the bar or bars, and wedge them into position with small wooden wedges.

Open up the lapping lead of the second panel, get it into position in the same way as the first, which you are putting on top of the first one, and lowering it gently over the top lead of the panel below. Mark the second saddle-bar's position and remove the second panel whilst you are cutting the saddle-bar holes. Replace the panel, wedge it, then place the saddle-bar in position and wedge that too. Continue in this until the whole window is built up to the *spring-line*.

When the spring-line and the shaped top of the stained glass are reached, owing to the width of the outer lead, the shaped top will not go flat-on into the tracery at the head of the window. Fold over the leads all round the outside of the glass, *both* leaves towards you, and gently easy the section into the correct position. To make this easier it is advisable to flange up the lapping lead so that it sticks out flat on both sides, and thus rides over the top lead of the preceding panel.

When the section is in position, straighten the leaf of the outside lead all round into the groove at the head of the window. It is essential to have a helper on the outside so that the panel can be supported between you until it is well wedged in position. You may be able to help support it yourself by putting an arm through a light or a tracery that has not yet been glazed.

Once all the sections are in position the next stage is to tie up each section to the appropriate bars with the copper wire ties that have been soldered on to the panels.

Section ties Thread the ties on the top panel down past the bar, on the far side, between the bar and the panel, and pull them down as far as they will go. Do the same thing in the opposite direction, i.e. upwards, still keeping them between the bar and the glass, to the ties on the bottom section. Bring each one round the bar, bottom and top, and twist them together with the pliers until they are quite firm.

Panel bars The copper ties in the centre section of the panel are wrapped round the bar to meet themselves and twisted and tightened. Only 12 mm to 19 mm ($\frac{1}{2}$ in. to $\frac{3}{4}$ in.) of twist need be left and the rest clipped off. The twists should be turned and laid flat along the bar.

By this time all the sections of the window will be pulled together securely, and firmly bound to the bars.

Now make certain that all the lap-leads are flanged down tight against the lower section. Under the outer flanges it is as well to put a small amount of blackened putty before finally flattening it down with a knife.

157 *Tracery lights in left hand window of Eton College Chapel, showing glass in position in the masonry prior to pointing up in mortar, 1959*

Pointing The final procedure is to point-up the window, using a mastic gun, but not too hastily, to thoroughly fill up all the holes and grooves. The mastic should be tidied up and smoothed with a small knife. When the mastic is three-quarters finished and fairly hard, remove the wooden wedges, and fill in the holes they leave.

The individual cusps of the tracery should be firmly fixed or made up at this stage. The penultimate thing is to clean down the whole window, and the last thing—which is forgotten only too often—is to remove the little pieces of labelling with the fixing numbers of the panels on them.*

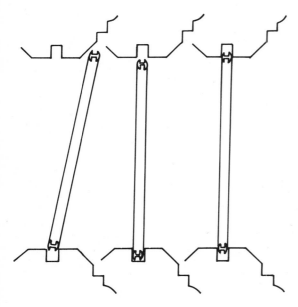

156 *Fixing: three stages in inserting panels into grooves in masonry*

* Some fixing numbers in Tours Cathedral can still be read twenty years after the glass has been replaced.

158 *Detail of window at Les Breseux, Jura, France. Designed by Alfred Manessier, executed by François Lorin 1954–5, showing method of French fixing*

159 *Exterior of Baptistry window, Coventry Cathedral, showing relationship of lead to the interstices of stonework*

160 *Detail of Coventry Cathedral nave windows, showing great weight of leading in contrast to the interstices of the stone*

Presentation in Exhibition

Often stained glass is put on exhibition in surroundings which are quite different to the normal siting of stained glass windows.

The best way to show glass, especially if it is largely unpainted, is to group a series of panels loosely around a central well of light—or let them stand on their own against a source of light, but at the same time let them be quite obviously separated from it.

In the case of very big panels of glass, the extent of the glass will be sufficient to dominate any excess light flowing round the edges, but with smaller panels it is best to put them into baffles whose side margins could be broader than those at the top and bottom, possibly with enough room to accommodate electric light, in the shape of a fluorescent strip, running down the back of them. Where there is no natural light, a white artificial light directed at a plain white wall behind the exhibit is best. The panels being separated from their source of light, add up to a far more convincing ensemble than if they are stuck on the wall isolated *from each other* in individual light-boxes.

Method of mounting

If the ceiling is low enough and the glass not too heavy the best way to mount a panel of stained glass is in a black baffle with a border of 102 mm (4 in.) or so, top and bottom, and 200 mm or 230 mm (8 in. or 9 in.) either side. The *baffle* may or may not have an inner baguette, like a frame of metal, actually to house the stained glass panel.

The glass should be fully polished and cleaned before putting it in the baffle, where it is lightly fixed with small but easily removable pins.

Lighting is mounted on the back of the baffle if needed. If fluorescent lighting is used, and it is preferable, remember that quite often coils, transformers, and starter motors have to be accommodated behind the baffle too—which is an added practical reason for having the baffle fairly broadly made.

The poles or rods to take the glass are made of any metal. I have found that square 1 in. by 1 in. mild steel tube, well cleaned with emery cloth and kept very slightly oiled, is the best and cheapest material. Holes for the screws to hold the baffle, are drilled beforehand, and corresponding holes are made in the baffle with a gimlet. A *grub-screw seating* is made at either end of the pole by welding a square nut into the square section of the pole. Two attachments, specially made out of a circular pad of metal with a grub-screw welded into the centre, are furnished with double octagonal nuts, so that when tightened they lock well.

Assembly is extremely quick. The horizontal distances between the poles supporting a baffle and between the individual exhibits are carefully plotted on the floor. The poles are put up by screwing the grub-screw at the bottom to nearly its fullest extension and leaving the top grub-screw with plenty of play. The panel should be mounted on the upright poles in the minimum time because of its weight and flimsiness, but the mounting is considerably speeded up by the drilling having been previously done. Any extra weight on the poles, as a result of mounting the glass, which might depress the floor and threaten the exhibit with an early death, can now be counteracted quickly by screwing up on the lee-way contained in the top grub-screw.

The electricity is now tackled. Take care to hide all wires and trailing flexes, and remember that the electricity takes as long to assemble and fix properly as the time taken in doing the rest of the exhibition. Anothing thing to remember is that flexes in the course of time tend to sag. One should check up from time to time to see that flex and cable do not show below the baffle. An exhibition 'with its slip showing' is a disgrace.

Another method of exhibiting is to have free-standing supports made to any design you like which are screwed on the baffle from the side. This method is, of course, almost forced on one where the lighting or the ceiling or the plan of the exhibition rooms is irregular. It is obviously a far more flexible method of setting out the exhibits than the previous one, but in the end does not really look quite as professional.

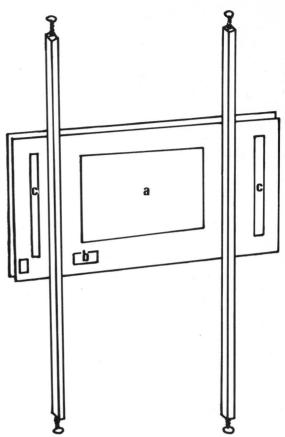

162 *Showing metal pipes supporting baffle seen from the back*
  a *glass*
  b *starter motor*
  c *fluorescent tubes*

161 *Exhibition pieces by Patrick Reyntiens showing method of mounting and display*

Artificially lit permanent panels

If the pieces of glass are large, and if they are not of obscured glass, they may well have to have a filter between the glass and the source of light in the form of a piece of opaque white plastic. This will have the effect of evening-out the light, and preventing the eye from penetrating beyond the surface of the glass. The only drawback to leaded glass in such a mural is that it may have to be braced behind the plastic by means of saddle-bars. In this case the plastic is first polished with de-statistising polish and fixed with a rubber-mastic adhesive on to the perimeter of the highly polished and scrupulously *well-cemented* stained glass. Holes are drilled in the plastic for the copper ties to come through, and these should tie onto a saddle-bar of suitable metal on *the other* side of the plastic. The holes that the copper ties come through are then sealed with a rubber latex compound, and the outer rim of glass and plastic, which has already been sealed together with rubber mastic, is again bound with masking tape (of the correct width, not to be seen from the outside of the glass).

The result is a panel which can be put into position, with a plastic diffusion unit on the back which never need be touched on the inside, between glass and plastic, and which will never be obscured by particles of dust.

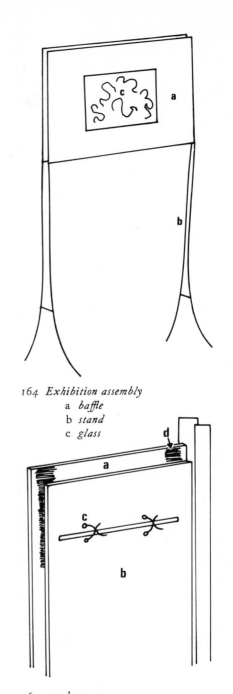

164 *Exhibition assembly*
    a *baffle*
    b *stand*
    c *glass*

163 *Grub screw attachment to poles top and bottom for exhibition*

165 a *glass*
    b *perspex diffuser*
    c *holes with copper ties protruding*
    d *mastic sealing compound*

Extended use of Antique and Thin Commercial Glass

Leaded glass is not the only way that stained glass can be made. Indeed, many people think that owing to the ecclesiastical overtones of leaded glass it can never be happily incorporated into the fabric of modern buildings. This is an extreme point of view: it *can* be done, but the success of the glass depends on the tonality and general '*ton*' or weight, of the colour scheme and the tonal pattern, and to a far greater extent on the sense of interval, the 'bigness' and 'smallness' of the individual pieces of glass.

The question of interval

Questions of interval in glass have not yet been fully investigated. This is curious, because one of the fundamental differences between thirteenth- and fourteenth-century glass, for instance, is the interval difference. The nature of modern architecture is such that it cannot digest random and intricate intervals such as are usually associated with stained glass.

Stained glass, of all art forms, is practically the only one which is still intimately incorporated in the actual *matière* of a building, and therefore the question of interval is a vital one.

It is in this situation that what have been called 'the extended uses of stained glass' come into their own. They provide a series of different finishes, qualities, textures, and light control, which are best displayed, not in the window embrasure, but in an extended role, as it were, of 'the precious object'. Having been divorced from architecture physically, they can fulfil their role in opposition to the architecture, or rather in counterpoint to it, and therefore make use of many techniques and visual effects of interval and colour that would be inappropriate if they were actually incorporated into the *matière* of a building.

Fused glass

If your kiln rises to a higher temperature than the average kiln, it is possible to fuse glass together, either in a series of pieces which are capable of being leaded together, which is not advisable because of the safety and durability of the end result, or, far better, in a series of pieces which could be incorporated in a composition of glass totally encapsuled in polyester or clear epoxy resin.*

Method of laying out

It is best to have a piece of plate glass as large as the total composition. If the composition is not in a flat plane, then bent plastic could be used in laying out, built up to the shape of the final stained glass.

* I should mention that the greatest exponent of fused glass techniques, to my mind, is Van Teterode of Amsterdam. He works on an heroic scale. The only work in England of his is at Pilkington's glass factory in St Helen's, Lancashire. From a technical point of view this is a staggering achievement. Van Teterode has interpreted Karel Appel into fused glass, and has also worked with Victor Pasmore.

Cutting The glass cutting may be done in the same way as in cutting antique, only a cutline is not a necessity. The glass is cut as the shape of the cartoon suggests, and then, perhaps, more glass is cut to modify the sharp visual edges of the pieces already cut. These pieces are placed on to the previous glass already in position, so that the act of cutting becomes, in effect, a form of improvisation on the theme suggested by the cartoon. It is in the technique of fused glass, more than any other technique, I feel, that the photographic cartoon might come into its own, because the very qualities that make it unsuited to the character of leaded stained glass and *dalle-de-verre* make it a real inspiration in fused glass. The subtle tone changes, the absence of definition and line, the melting quality of one passage into another, the slow elision of one colour into another, the accidental dots and blotches. All these can be translated and heightened and developed in a fused glass technique.

Attaching the glass Unless the stained glass composition is on a curve, the best way to fix the glass is with blobs of plasticine, as in leaded glass, though these should be very small. Once all the building up has been done, it is as well to turn the glass so that the back of the plate glass is towards you in the studio, and the cut antique to the light. Suspend a tracing paper on the back and sketch through it the positions of the glass as they overlay each other. The tracing paper should be drawn out exactly to size, and have an accurate, though skeleton, tracing on it of the principal areas of the composition. In this way, when the position has been plotted the glass can be dismounted and laid on the trays of the kiln with a reasonable amount of accuracy and fired at a very high temperature. The act of laying the glass in its exact position on the plaster is most important and is perhaps *the* point of decision as to whether the end result is a work of art or not.

If lead is used in bonding the final glass together, great care should be taken over the edges of the individual pieces. Obviously they must be capable of being glazed once they have been fired. Perhaps the best way, but not the only way, is to cut thick glass templates to the size and shape of the intervals in the tracing paper and place your glass down to be fused on these. The hazards are two-fold: (1) the plate glass and antique glass develop lesions. (2) Even if they do not, the difficulty in ensuring complete continuity from one piece to the next, is very great; nearly always, in leading up, there is a slight jerk or hiatus from one passage of glass to another where they do not exactly correspond, which can be visually disturbing.

In fused glass, all the techniques of aciding and painting can be used on the glass prior to fusing. In the case of painting, the paint can be incorporated to unify with the glass, actually during the fusing process.

It is important to realise beforehand, however, how glass is likely to behave at very high temperatures and many experiments will be necessary.

Behaviour of glass

Reds Selenium reds sometimes turn yellowish, but if previously stained a little, only modify to a leonine red. Copper reds, being flashed, while perfectly retaining their colour, tend physically to distort, showing a white rim all round the red colour which retreats further to the centre of the glass the more you heat it. The thicker the base of white glass, the more likelihood there is of the white rim showing. This can have its advantages, but if you want to avoid it cut the flash face-down.

Blues and greens All blues and greens retain their colour in the fire. The behaviour of pot glass is very good: flashed glass may develop a white ring round it, like the red, for exactly the same reasons. Greens are liable to sulphur heavily. This can be removed on the outside by mopping with hydrofluoric acid after fusing, using great care, but nothing can be done to greens if sulphuring occurs between two layers of fused glass.

White and yellow fuse very well. Care should be taken when changing the plaster before firing, in case it retains any stain within it. Hidden stain, a residue lurking in the plaster from continuous stain fires, will pock mark and spot any glass that is fused together on top of it. Naturally the whites and the yellows are the most susceptible to this.

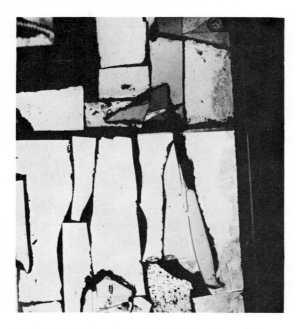

166 *Three details of resin and antique glass windows by Keith New and Tom Fairs showing characteristic sharpness of silhouettes of individual pieces in this technique*

Other colours Most other colours fuse well. Generally speaking the thinner the sheet, the more easy the act of fusing.

Some greens and yellows are exceptionally malleable; they melt, running into more stable pieces of glass. They should perhaps be put on top of the other pieces of glass, rather than underneath when fusing.

Stain cannot be used in fused glass as it invariably goes so dark that it usually turns out as a black blot. Fused glass, if leaded, needs extra specially strong and stable leads.

Fused glass in polyester resin
If fused glass is totally incorporated into polyester resin, the effect can be very attractive. The main advantage, apart from the purely practical one of not allowing the glass to start disintegrating, is that the rather disparate effect between the softness of the edges in the glass, and the harsh network of lines made by the heavy leading (in the previous method) is eliminated. The individual pieces of fused glass can be a random shape but can be joined together effectively, from an artistic point of view, by the superimposition of flatter, thinner pieces of fused glass which tend to disguise the harshness of the changeover line.

Glass overlaid by polyester resin

This method of using simple, individual pieces of glass, is easier, less expensive and far less tedious than the fused glass technique. On the other hand, the edge values of compositions done in simple overlaid glass are not nearly as soft and poetic as those of fused glass. However you treat it, glass in polyester resin suffers from a sharpness in edge value and a feeling of irritating jagged pieces which is very difficult to eliminate from an artistic, and from a practical, point of view. Before being cast in polyester the glass may be painted, stained, fired, and acided in the same way as leaded glass. It is mounted, either horizontally on a large flat table, or vertically upon an easel of plate glass in the same way as fused glass is, i.e. by means of an accurate skeleton tracing, on tracing paper instead of a cutline on tracing linen. Like fused glass, the process of cutting is really a direct amplification of the cartoon, and there is a good deal of inspired improvisation about it.

Method

When all the glass is assembled on the light table in the right order, it is transferred to a mould the exact size and shape of the finished panel.

The mould

Depending on what shape the stained glass composition is going to be, the mould can be made of many things; it can, if the composition is curved, be made of shellac-painted plaster of Paris—or it could be made of formica or rubber sheeting on hardboard or metal. The corners and cracks along the edges of the mould should be well sealed off. Sheet polythene is not recommended, simply because, although it has many advantages (of non-adhesion, transparency, and durability) the great disadvantage is that, whatever happens, it gathers into folds and bumps under the resin during the process of casting. Absolutely nothing can be done about this, so unless you are happy to have a random ripple over the whole composition, I do not advise it. Acrilic sheet or plastic has the advantage that it is transparent and rigid and is most probably the best base for a mould. If an acrilic mould is laid directly on the light table

and the pieces of glass are cut and built up in the mould in their final position, they will not need to be moved, and the composition, which depends as much on chance inspiration as on careful forethought, will retain its freshness and vitality.

Placing the glass in the mould

The question of complete encapsulation of the glass in the polyester resin is most important.

In casting glass into polyester the main things to remember are (1) the undesirability of bubbles getting under the glass when the mould is being filled with the liquid resin; (2) the limited time allowed for casting, because of the short viscous life of the resin.

These two factors are intimately linked. If the glass is complicated it should be put into the mould layer by layer, almost at the same time as the polyester resin is mixed. To do this, the glass waiting to be used can be separated out, layer from layer, by means of an interleaving of glass or perspex. In this way the various layers of glass making up the design can be separated and made to come together with the minimum amount of labour and time-wasting when the casting operation actually begins.

In casting, it is best to have two people working together, one to attend to the glass, one to attend to the resin. There should be enough room in the studio to spread out the various layers of glass, all correctly laid out in order, and within easy reach. There should be a *small table* on wheels, with the weighing machine, the resin, the hardener and any colouring matter, releasing agent, rods for mixing, and a prick for dealing with bubbles. It is best to mix sufficient resin to cover the whole base area of the composition first, enough to cover to a depth of 6–9 mm ($\frac{1}{4}$–$\frac{3}{8}$ in.) depending obviously on the eventual size and weight of the panel you are doing. The resin must be used at once, before it gets to the critical stage of its chemical combination, and it must not be allowed to remain in the pouring container many minutes; otherwise it is more than liable to turn white-hot and have to be dealt with by means of a pair of tongs, and rushed into the garden. When the mould has been evenly

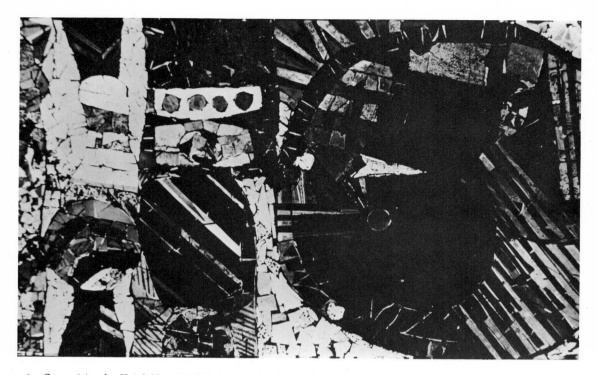

167 *Composition by Keith New ARCA, in resin-bonded antique glass*

filled to 6 mm ¼ in., place the first layer of the glass on the resin, when it will half sink into the resin, but stand proud a little. More resin should then be mixed and then poured, so that it is just covering the glass. A second layer of glass can be put on—more resin mixed, and a third layer put on. All the layers of glass should have been thoroughly cleaned with alcohol or acetone to begin with, well before starting the casting process, and should be perfectly dry.

Finally, a full layer of polyester resin as a sealer should be floated over the whole composition, to make the inside face as smooth, if possible, as the outer. When the polyester resin has set enough, it is possible to smooth it, plane it, and polish it to a high gloss.

Points to note

1 The resin becomes viscous very quickly. Obviously it is an advantage to work with the resin when it is most liquid, but with patience and experience the distances between layers of glass can be varied by the *amount* of resin used in combination with the timing of the placing of the glass, after the resin has been poured.

2 If possible, the casting should always be done on a light-table, so that you can see what you are doing the whole time. Quite often compositions which look right when laid out on the table without the resin, are apt to look thin and lack punch when they have been surrounded with resin. This is something to do with the variations in light-refraction propensity. As a parallel phenomenon,

experiment with a prism from a chandelier; put it into water and notice how it loses its sparkle; the principle is the same in glass surrounded by polyester resin. One remedy for this, when it occurs, is to have a cutting bench or table by you, with supplementary pieces of glass (they may be odd pieces of stained, painted, or acided glass), and use a quick cut of glass as an improvisation to enrichen any passages that look meagre. Alternatively, you could have a tray of glass already cut, of the right colour and an appropriate size, by your side, and simply add as you go ahead with the casting.

Additional points concerning polyester

When casting fused glass on to polyester, it is as well to give the individual fused glass an injection of liquid polyester between the glass layers, as, if they have not quite fused together in a solid lump, there will inevitably be holes and spaces between the pieces of glass. The best way of doing this is to have a supply of deep (at least 30 cm   1 ft) polythene bags similar to the kind used for deep-freezing. Pour the polyester, immediately it is mixed, into the bag, then, either by pricking or cutting off the corner, and screwing up the loose end of the bag and squeezing it like an icing bag, sufficient pressurized polyester can be poured into the smallest crevices between the glass. The glass should be dry and clean, and it is advisable to wear rubber gloves, as well as remembering *not* to exceed the critical amount of polyester in the polythene bag.

Polyester resin itself can be coloured with a large range of dyes that can themselves be mixed. These can be obtained from many an artist's colourman. These can be used in combination with actual stained glass in as many ways as you fancy, but in the end the two systems, which are a feasible physical possibility together, hardly mix happily from the point of view of art. Black polyester or a very dark colour, used sparingly, like paint in ordinary stained glass, either to separate colours or to modify them, is licit. The *artistic* and *practical* drawbacks of these three methods of using polyester resin are:

1 *Artistic* Theoretically, the use of polyester, because it means unlimited expanse of window space without leading or mullion interruption, is very attractive. In actual fact the result is not too convincing, largely because of the question of interval on the eye. In distinction to leaded glass, where the intervals can be too small and too irritating, there is no practical reason for interval to play any part in polyester resin glass at all. In consequence, the introduction of a mullion comes as a pretty large artistic impertinence. But, on the other hand, if you use no mullions in polyester windows, the compositions—having no rigid definition of division or interval—are apt to change their character and become mere transparencies, transferring the *picture interest* from the wall to the window. Transparencies always give the mind an uneasy feeling that it is being 'got at' in an immoral way—the object contemplated is not quite a window, and not quite a painting: it is an artistic hermaphrodite, a will-jill. This is a truism in leaded glass, but the chances of falling into this trap in stained glass are minimal compared with the possibilities of artistic gaffes in polyester resin. What would the illusion-mongers of the eighteenth century have given for the possibilities of polyester resin?

2 *Practical* I have yet to be convinced that polyester resin of the highest quality is really weather-resistant for the length of time that leaded glass has been proved to be. This is one more reason why the employment of polyester in windows is not, perhaps, the best use to which it can be put. Of course, windows can be, and are, double-glazed, and a plate glass outside a polyester window is an enormous improvement in *matière*. It immediately eliminates on the outside of a building, the slightly viscid look of the artificial resin which, although capable of taking a high polish, still manages to look uncomfortably *plastic*. The best use of polyester, both artistically and practically, remains in its role of a 'precious object' within a clearly defined space, suspended or removed from the actual *matière* of the building.

Safety precautions

All artificial resins are potentially dangerous to health. Not only in direct contact with the hands and other parts of the body, but in dust form when breathed in during such operations as polishing, grinding down, and sawing. The only casualties that I have ever known have all been traced back to two things—inadequate ventilation and careless handling.

Ventilation is very important, as the fumes given off by some of the hardeners are increased when the resin, having been mixed, gets hot. The fumes are attracted to water, and make a bee-line for any of the more watery parts and passages. Severe external and internal dermatitis can result.

Since resins set best at a mean temperature of about 60°C (dependent on the resin), mixing and casting outside is out of the question. Therefore the only thing to do is to have a forced extraction ventilator fitted up, not only within easy reach of where you mix and cast, but also near where the panel is finally going to harden off.

The use of disposable containers for the mixed resin helps minimise the dangers of dermatitis, by largely eliminating the use of solvents to clean the containers, because solvents can cause dermatitis too.

Rubber gloves can be a snare and a delusion, because if any resin is picked up inside the glove, the sweat from the hands provides ideal conditions for developing dermatitis. Wrists, elbows, and hands should be covered with the right sort of barrier-cream, then the overall should be pulled well down. If rubber gloves are used, they should be bound under the overall sleeves with masking tape. Do not get the barrier-cream near the eyes.

Wear a mask and goggles when polishing or smoothing down resin.

Use the new types of resin-cleansing creams on the skin, not the crude solvents.

The usual rules of cleanliness in the studio will eliminate much of the possibility of accidents.

Spontaneous combustion

Polyester resins, especially, are spontaneously combustible in conjunction with organic substances such as turps, alcohol, meths, and acetone, and these should be kept well away from one another. Polyester resins are very often in solution with certain chemicals which make for spontaneous combustion when mixed with hardener, even if not in a critical mass (rather over 50 mm 2 in. cube), if they are allowed to remain in odd cloths, etc., lying around the studio. Get rid of the lot, including any resin left over from the casting operation, into a bin outside; damp the cloths before putting them into the bin.

Fibreglass and Polyester Resin

In addition to the method of casting fused glass and layers of antique glass in polyester, there is a method of using layers of fibreglass to bond antique glass together so as to form a window. Whereas in the previous methods it is usual to incorporate the glass totally into the resin, by using fibreglass it is possible to leave both faces of the glass free of resin.

Tools
1 An accurate balance.
2 Containers; tin or glass or plastic.
  Plastic containers can be retained and cleaned.
3 Rods for mixing. Prick for releasing air bubbles.
  Old brushes.
  Washered rollers of various widths.
  Any amount of old rags or tissues.
4 Protective clothing, rubber gloves, and goggles.

Materials
1 The usual resins, accelerators, catalysts, and hardeners. There are a variety of makes of polyester resin. All the catalysts and hardeners should come from the same source of supply as the polyester resin.
2 Silicone polish, releasing agent, cleansing solution, and barrier cream.
  After preparing the cartoon draw the outline so that the gaps between the glass are far more pronounced and bolder than in leaded glass. The outline has very much the same role of discipline as the outline in leaded glass, and compositions executed in fibreglass and polyester resin have none of the flexibility of approach or the random freedom of the two previous methods of using polyester resin.

Method
First prepare a horizontal surface, rather larger than the eventual composition, with a wax silicone polish and then coat with a releasing agent. On another table conveniently handy, have a series of templates of fibreglass sheeting, which have all been carefully cut to the shape of the outline, leaving holes in exactly the right place and pattern to correspond to the sizes and shapes of the glass.

Cutting the fibreglass
1 Lay the fibreglass on a table which has a linoleum surface.
2 When cutting out the fibreglass allow a good margin all round the perimeter of the composition, so that the fibreglass can be trimmed to size with a fine-toothed saw when it has hardened.
3 Take a tracing of the outline in tracing paper and lay it on top of as many layers of fibreglass as you will need.
4 Nail battens round the perimeter within the area of the fibreglass, but outside the area of the composition.
5 With a well-sharpened glazing knife and a small hammer cut through the tracing paper and the fibreglass vertically, tapping the knife with the hammer. Have a well sharpened pen-knife or scalpel handy for finishing off the cutting.

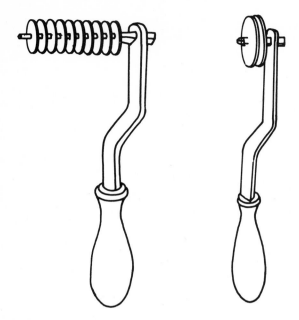

168 *Roller for breaking and bonding fibreglass in use with polyester resin*

The amount of fibreglass to be cut should be the same thickness as the glass employed—usually 3 mm–4 mm ($\frac{1}{8}$ in.–$\frac{3}{15}$ in.) but the thickness of fibreglass may have to be increased up to ($\frac{1}{4}$ in. 6 mm or $\frac{3}{8}$ in. 9 mm) if the size of the panel is considerable.

Mixing resin

The formulas for mixing the resin vary slightly according to their manufacture. You must obey the manufacturer's instructions. For pure resin a proportion of 454 g (1 lb) resin to 2% by weight of hardener is the usual amount. But if a filler is used the proportion changes to 454 g (1 lb) resin to 2% to 4% of hardener by weight. An average mix has a life of about twenty minutes.

Remember the more you have in bulk the more it is likely to explode or ignite, but a *shallow* container reduces this risk considerably.

Making the panel

Paint the surface of the casting area with a gell coat of resin, making sure that the coating is even all over. Lay on the first layer of fibreglass and roll it with the roller specially made for fibre-

glass. This breaks the fibres and makes them bond well together in the polyester resin. When the first layer of fibreglass is well bonded in the resin, lay the glass (which can have been previously stained, painted, and acided just as in leaded glass) in the corresponding gaps left in the fibreglass. Next coat the fibreglass that is already in position with resin, and lay on the second layer of fibreglass; roll this very thoroughly so that it unites with the first layer in a matt.

Proceed in exactly the same way, layer by layer, until the fibreglass, well pressed down, is the same thickness as the glass. Where the glass varies in thickness you may find that it is necessary to build up the fibreglass with small scraps left over from the cutting to bring it up to the required level. Finish off with a generous coating of resin and allow to harden.

Notes

1 Apply the resin with an old brush and dab it rather than stroke it on.
2 A releasing agent should be used on either face of the glass if it is required to end up quite clean. Never allow the releasing agent to go over the side of the glass, as this will prevent the glass and the resin from uniting.
3 While in the process of doing the laminating it is inevitable that some stray strands of fibre glass will go across the surface of the glass. This may well add to the quality of the design but if it is not wanted the strands must be pushed to the edge of the pieces of glass as soon as they appear. Releasing agent on the glass, of course, obviates having to do this.
4 Always pay attention to the corners and small areas of fibre.
5 When using the washered roller be very careful that you do not move the pieces of glass out of position.
6 When applying several layers of fibreglass, allow every pair to gell in sequence before continuing with another layer. This is necessary in order to avoid the composition buckling and bowing. When finished, the surface of the fibreglass can be polished or ground or painted as is required.

Detail from Wendling showing the effect of designing in collage and translated into glass. See page 32

Bibliography

Technical

Art of Glass Painting	C. Winston	John Murray London 1865
The Art and Craft of Stained Glass	E. W. Twining	Pitman & Sons 1928
L'Art de La Peinture sur Verre et de la Vitrerie	M. le Vieil	Paris 1774
Stained Glass Work	C. H. Whall	John Hogg London 1905
Hints on Glass Painting	Parts 1 and 2 Anon	Parker Oxford 1847

Historical

The Norwich School of Glass Painting	C. Woodforde	Oxford University Press 1950
The Stained Glass of New College, Oxford	C. Woodforde	Oxford University Press 1951
English Stained and Painted Glass	C. Woodforde	Clarendon Press 1954
Irish Stained Glass	James White and Michael Wynne	
		The Furrow Trust Dublin 1963
Windows: A book about stained glass	Lewis F. Day	Batsford 1909
Les Vitraux de la Cathédrale de Chartres	Text and Vols 1, 2, 3 L'Abbé Delaporte	
		E. Houvet Chartres 1926
Ancient Stained and Painted Glass	F. Sydney Eden	
		Cambridge University Press 1933
Corpus Vitriarum Medii Aevi		
Vitraux de France, eleventh to fifteenth century	Louis Grodecki	Caisse Nationalle des Monuments Historiques
The Painted Glass of York	F. Harrison	SPCK 1927
Stained Glass of York Minster	F. Harrison	The Studio Ltd London
The York School of Glass Painting	John F. Knowles	1936
Musée Retrospectif de la classe '67 Vitraux	M. Lucien Magne	
Italian Stained Glass Windows	G. Marchini	
		Thames & Hudson London 1957
Ancient Glass of Canterbury Cathedral	Bernard Rackham	Lund Humphries
English Stained Glass	Herbert Read	Putnams London 1926
Les Vitraux de la Cathédrale de Rouen	George Ritter	Cognac 1926
Stained Glass Tours in France	Charles Hitchcock Sherrill	
		John Lane London 1909
Stained Glass Tours in England	Charles Hitchcock Sherrill	
		John Lane Bodley Head 1909

159

Stained Glass Tours in Italy Charles Hitchcock Sherrill
John Lane Bodley Head 1913

Stained Glass Tours in Spain and Flanders Charles Hitchcock Sherrill
John Lane Bodley Head 1924

Stained Glass Tours in Austria, Germany and The Rhinelands Charles Hitchcock Sherrill
John Lane Bodley Head 1927

The Lost Art R. Sowers Zwemmer
Stained Glass: An Architectural Art R. Sowers Zwemmer
Stained Glass of the Middle Ages Hugh Arnold Black London 1913
Stained Glass Windows V. Beyer Oliver & Boyd London 1964
Vitraux de Bourges S. Clement A. Guitard
Tardy-Pigelet Bourges 1900

Adventures in Light and Colour Charles Connick Harrap 1937
The Stained Glass of William Morris and His Circle A. C. Sewter Yale University Press 1975

Antiquarian
A History of Design in Painted Glass Vols I, II, III, and IV
N. H. J. Westlake James Parker 1894

A History of English Glass Painting Maurice Drake
T. Werner Laurie Ltd London 1912

Folio. Vitraux Peints Cathédrale de Mans Eugene Hucher Didron Paris 1965
Histoire de la Painture sur Verre Vols. 1 & 2 Ferdinand de Lasteyrie
Didot Freres Paris 1853

Vitraux de France Twelfth and Thirteenth Century Jean Verrier Histoire des Arts Plastiques Paris
Les Verriers de la Cathédrale de Tours C. H. Boissonnet Paris 1932
The Jerusalem Windows Marc Chagall. Text, J. Leymarie
André Sauret Monaco 1962

English Stained Glass Herbert Read Putnams London 1926
Swiss Stained Glass of the Fourteenth Century Michael Stettler Batsford 1949
Stained Glass Twelfth and Thirteenth Century French Cathedrals Marcel Aubert Batsford 1951
English Stained Glass J. Baker, A. Lammer
Thames & Hudson 1960

Vitraux de la Cathédrale de Strasbourg Paul Ahnne, Victor Beyer Strasbourg 1960

Glossary

Aciding	Process of etching the 'flash' off antique glass
Aggregate	Inert granular material mixed with cement to make concrete
Antique Glass	Sheet glass produced by the process of glass blowing. Used mostly in production of stained glass
Armature	Structure, usually of metal, used within the concrete for strengthening
Ballast	See aggregate
Banding	Action of fixing copper wire to panels of glass
Cartoon	Working painting or drawing, usually full-sized
Chamber Annealing	That part of the kiln which is used to cool down fired glass
Collage	Method of producing area of colour on paintings of cartoons, usually coloured paper, cut to required shape and stuck on to the cartoon
Cusping	Small protruding points of stone within areas of Gothic tracery
Cutline	Tracing, usually on linen, showing the positions and juxtapositions of pieces of glass
Delcalcomania	The action of blotting with paper or other such substance a wet layer of paint. The paper is then removed and a random pattern results. This is also known as 'tonking'.
Dalle-de-Verre	French term for inch-thick glass. Literally— 'paving stone of glass'
Ferrule	Ruler
Fraille	Frame used for transporting glass
Flash Glass	Two-coloured glass, usually antique, one colour being very much thinner than the other
Galvanic Action	Electrolytic action between two different metals in close proximity, having degenerative effect on the metals
Gamboge	Yellow pigment. An ingredient of silver stain
Grozer	Tool used in shaping and cutting glass
Knapping	Same as knapping flints. A sideways tap, shelling the edges of *dalle-de-verre* to create glitter and sparkle through refraction
Laitance	The shiny residue of cement left after casting concrete has been vibrated. From the French meaning 'soft herring roe'

Laminating	Process of building up thickness with resin and fibreglass
Lathekin	Pronounced and sometimes spelt Larriken, Lathikin, Lathiken. Tool made of wood or bone for manipulating lead calmes
Lead Calmes	Strip of lead milled to a specified shape and size. Can be spelt calm or came
Muller	Small hand mill made of glass or marble for grinding paint powder very finely on a pallette
Mullion	Vertical inner division of window used in Gothic architecture to uphold the inner tracery of windows. Wooden verticals used in the studio to represent the above and to support easels
Mushroom	In stained glass, the emergence of cement in a mushroom shape between two pieces of glass
Marbling	Method of getting random pattern on glass, either with paint or stopping-out agent prior to aciding
Oil of Spike	Solvent for enamel medium
Pinhole	Small holes appearing as defects in fully painted glass
Pounce Bag	Small cloth bag filled with whitening
Pyrometer	A thermometer for registering very high temperatures usually through platinum resistance to electricity
Rovings	Spun glass threads any number of which together increase the tensile strength of a panel of epoxy resin and glass
Shuttering	Wooden sides to cast concrete or epoxy moulds
Spatula	Flexible mixing knife for paint
Springline	The horizontal line below which the upright sides end and above which the curve of the arch begins
Straight-edge	Heavy metal rule of perfectly milled edge, unmarked with intervals
Striations	Marks on antique glass, like scratches, making the glass more brilliant and crystalline in effect
Scribe	Instrument for incising a line in *dalle-de-verre*, usually a steel wheel
Stippling	Method of painting using the butt end of the brush, usually a badger, to let in minute points of light through the paint
Template	Shape, cut out of tracing paper, paper, or thin glass corresponding to the exact size of a piece of glass required
Tinning	Action of coating the soldering copper with tin
Tracery	Shapes in the head of a Gothic window
Whipping	The action of fanning paint with the badger

Suppliers

Great Britain

Bronze Fixing	Harris & Edgar Ltd, 21 Gurney Road, Carshalton, Surrey
Ceramic Colours Chemical	Wengers Ltd, Stoke-on-Trent, Staffs
	Griffin & George Ltd, Ealing Road, Alperton, Middlesex
Glass	James Hetley & Co Ltd, Beresford Avenue, Wembley, Middlesex
Lead	Lonsdale Metal Co Ltd, 608 High Road, London E10
Lead Milling Machinery and Soldering Irons	Sharratt & Newth Ltd, c/o Van Moppes and Son Ltd, Winchester Road, Basingstoke, Hants
Lead Vices	Johnson Matthey, 78 Hatton Gardens, London EC1
Glass-cutting Machinery	Sharratt & Newth Ltd, c/o Van Moppes and Son Ltd, Winchester Road, Basingstoke, Hants
Paper	Harper & Tunstall Ltd, Leto Works, High Street, Edgeware, Middlesex
	Ibico Paper, Brown of the Mound, Edinburgh
Perspex	Suntex Ltd, Iver, Bucks
	G. H. Bloore Ltd, Edgware, Middlesex
Plaster of Paris	Gyproc Ltd, Ferguson House, Marylebone Road, London NW1
Putty and Whitening	Dussek Brothers, Oil and Rosin Refiners, Thames Road, Crayford, Kent
Soldering Sticks, Soldering Irons	James Hetley & Co Ltd, Beresford Avenue, Wembley, Middlesex
Stains and Paints	James Hetley & Co Ltd, Beresford Avenue, Wembley, Middlesex
	Johnson Matthey & Co, Ceramics Division, 78 Hatton Gardens, London EC1
Tools in General	Buck & Ryan Ltd, 101 Tottenham Cort Road, London W1
Welding Equipment	British Oxygen Co, East Lane, North Wembley, Middlesex

U.S.A.

Blow torches

The Otto Bernz Co.,
  280 Lyell Avenue, Rochester 6, N.Y.

Copper sheet

Chase Brass & Copper Co.
  (Offices in most cities)

Enamels

Art-Brite Color & Chemicals, Manufacturers,
  19 La Grange Street, Brooklyn, N.Y. 11206

Nesbert L. Cochran,
  2540 So. Fletcher Avenue, Fernandina
  Beach, Florida

Foils, silver and gold

Wehrung & Billmeier Co.,
  3624 Lincoln Avenue, Chicago, Ill.

Jewelry findings

American Metalcraft Inc.,
  4100 Belmont Avenue, Chicago 41, Ill.

Kilns

Electric Hotpak Co.,
  Coltman Avenue at Melrose St, Philadelphia,
  Penna.

Ferro Corporation,
  4150 East 56 Street, Cleveland, Ohio

Tools and equipment

Allcraft Tool & Supply Co.,
  11 East 48 Street, New York, N.Y. 10017

Edward Winter,
  University Circle, 11020 Magnolia Drive,
  Cleveland, Ohio

General Dealers

Bergen Arts & Crafts,
  Salem, Mass.

Immerman's Crafts Inc.,
  16912 Miles Street, Cleveland, Ohio

St Louis Crafts Inc.,
  St Louis 19, Mo.

Thomas C. Thompson Co.,
  1539 Old Dearfield Road, Highland Park, Ill.

*The dealers listed above supply a range of
materials and equipment for enamelling*

Enamels, kilns, basic equipment, and supplies

Allcraft Tool and Supply Co., Inc
100 Frank Road
Hicksville, NY 11801

American Art Clay Co
4717 West 16th Street
Indianapolis, IN 46222

Kraft Korner
5842 Mayfield Road
Cleveland, OH 44124

Sax Arts and Crafts
P.O.B. 2002
Milwaukee, WI 53201

Thomas C. Thompson
1539 Deerfield Road
Highland Park, IL 60035

Triarco Arts and Crafts
J. C. Larson Co
7330 North Clark Street
Chicago, IL 60626

U.S. Lapidary Supply Company, Inc
1605 West San Carlos
San Jose, CA 95128

Western Ceramics Supply Co
1601 Howard Street
San Francisco, CA 94103

Special Sources

American Metalcraft, Inc
4100 West Belmont Avenue
Chicago, IL 60641
(copper panels and shapes and enamelling tools)

Carpenter and Wood Co, Inc
15 Cedar Street
Providence, R.I. 02903
(jeweler's enamels)

The Ceramic Coating Co
P.O.B. 310
Newport, KY 41072
(leadless enamels)

Norbert L. Cochran
2540 Fletcher Avenue
Fernandina Beach, FL 32034
(Distributor for Schauer and Co of Vienna, Austria—special enamels and supplies)

Seaire
17909 South Hobart Street
Gardena, CA 90248
(wire-brushed copper panels and shapes, special tools, racks, enamels, and other supplies)

Kilns only

J. J. Cress Co, Inc
1718 Floradale Avenue
South El Monte, CA 91733

Ludd Vcella
11482 Pipeline
Pomona, CA 91766

Miscellaneous Supplies

Abrasives (carborundum, emery paper and pumice): hardware stores

Acid: chemical suppliers, pharmacies and enameling suppliers

Copper: (sheet) industrial metal suppliers listed in telephone directories; (sheet, shapes, and panels) enameling suppliers; (tooling foil) metal suppliers, craft and hobby stores

Lacquers and waxes: hardware stores

Propane hand torches and asbestos products: hardware stores

Index